A COMPLIMENTARY REVIEW COPY, FALL 1968

A DEFENDERS OF FREEDOM BOOK

Dwight David Eisenhower: Fighter for Peace

BY COL. "RED" REEDER
ILLUSTRATED BY CARY

ABOUT THE BOOK: The life of one of the most important men of our time is given real meaning in this exciting life story of Dwight D. Eisenhower, who became known as the "man of peace." His life, from childhood on, is covered here in colorful detail, and reflects the man's hard work, determination, warmth, and humor. Special attention is given to his leadership and accomplishments during World War II. This is one of Garrard's new *DEFENDERS OF FREEDOM* books, which bring to life fascinating characters, both contemporary and historical, and reconstruct with vivid detail and action many of the important crises in history.

Subject classification: Social Studies, American History, Biography
Sub-classification: World War II, Military History, Reading, Information

ABOUT THE AUTHOR: Col. "Red" Reeder has been associated with the Army all his life. He was an outstanding athlete at West Point and directed athletics for the Army in the Canal Zone. He began writing seriously after he was sent to Guadalcanal in 1942. His report of his trip, entitled "Fighting on Guadalcanal," was a classic of war reporting. More than one million copies of it were printed and were used as training manuals. His military service extended until his retirement in 1947. He led a regiment ashore in Normandy on D-Day and was seriously wounded on the sixth day of the invasion. For 20 years he served as Special Assistant to the Director of Athletics at West Point. He is the author of more than 24 books.

Reading Level: Grade 5   Interest Level: Grades 4–7
160 pages . . . 6⅞ x 9⅛   Publisher's Price: $2.98

Illustrated with photographs and 2-color art; full-color jacket; reinforced binding; index

GARRARD PUBLISHING COMPANY

GETTYSBURG.
PENNSYLVANIA

I have learned that my old friend Colonel Red Reeder is writing, for the use of young readers, a short biography of my life. Knowing Red from the days of World War II, in which he was one of our gallant fighting men, I am sure that his book will be both readable and factual.

Dwight D. Eisenhower

DWIGHT DAVID
EISENHOWER

Fighter for Peace

BY COLONEL "RED" REEDER

ILLUSTRATED BY CARY

GARRARD PUBLISHING COMPANY
CHAMPAIGN, ILLINOIS

FOR

Narcissa Martin Reeder Whitehouse

And Her Children

Julia Reeder Summerall
Fred Martin Reeder
Nardi Reeder Campion

And Her Grandchildren

Charles P. Summerall III
Julia Summerall Smith
Ann Reeder Riggs
Dorothea Reeder Hruby
Charles Green Reeder
Julia Reeder McCutchen
Russell P. Reeder III
Thomas B. Campion Jr.
Edward W. Campion
Frederick C. Campion
Narcissa Campion
Russell Reeder Campion

And Her Great-grandchildren

Margi Smith
John C. Smith III
Robert Bruce Smith
Jenny Summerall
Virginia Riggs
Dale E. Hruby II
Charles P. Summerall IV
Dorothea Hruby
Philip R. Riggs
Charles Smith
Julia Smith
Alan J. McCutchen II
Elizabeth Hruby
Dorothea Riggs
Heather McCutchen
Wendy Reeder
Thomas G. Summerall

Photo Credits:

Authenticated News International: p. 11
Dwight David Eisenhower Library, Abilene, Kansas: p. 13, 14, 44, 70, 144, 147, 153
United Press International: p. 50, 55, 137, 143, 149
United States Army: p. 2, 21, 63, 79, 82, 87, 90, 92, 99, 108, 111, 117, 120, 124, 125
United States Coast Guard: p. 107
United States Military Academy Archives: p. 24, 36, 40, 128
United States Navy, National Archives: p. 65
Weyand, A. M.: p. 30
White House Collection: p. 138
Wide World: p. 57, 67, 97, 103, 130, 133, 139, 141, 156

Maps by Henri A. Fluchere

J
923.1
E

Contents

1. All Aboard for West Point   7

2. In Cadet Uniform   21

3. On the Army Team   32

4. After Graduation   40

5. The Fox Who Could Teach   48

6. The Hurricane Breaks   57

7. Teamwork   71

8. Fighting in Africa   78

9. "You Won't Have a Friend Left"   92

10. D-Day 101

11. Normandy 109

12. The German Salute 117

13. "I Like Ike" 127

14. The President Who Fought for Peace . . 138

15. Fifty Stars 149

    Index 158

1. All Aboard for West Point

The bell on the iron monster clanged. The engineer slammed on the brakes, and the Union Pacific train rattled to a stop.

"Abilene!" the conductor shouted.

The conductor stepped off the train and placed an iron step on the platform to aid his passengers. The engine wheezed and puffed as if it were out of breath from its run across the Kansas prairies. The station platform was crowded, for most people traveled by train in 1911.

On the edge of the crowd stood six boys who had come to tell young Dwight D. Eisenhower good-bye.

One boy said: "Ike, I can just see you in a football uniform at West Point. I know you'll play on the Army team. Good luck!"

Another said: "I hear the Military Academy is a tough place, especially for first year plebes. The upperclassmen are rough on 'em. What about that, Ike?"

Dwight Eisenhower grinned. He had a smile that made you glad you were with him. "I'm not worried about upperclassmen," he said.

"All aboard!" the conductor called. "Step lively, please! 'Board for Junction City, Kansas City, and points east!"

Zipping around the corner of the station came Flip, Ike's white fox terrier. Flip was a trick dog. She pranced on her hind legs, her front paws hanging limp. Seeing her made Ike laugh. He was glad to laugh at this moment. "Go on home, Flip," Ike said. "Beat it!"

The bell on the engine began to toll. "Ike" Eisenhower shook hands hurriedly with his friends, picked up his suitcase, and ran up the iron steps into the day coach.

The train jerked forward. Eisenhower pressed his face against the window for a farewell look at Abilene. He hated leaving his family. He knew that if he made good at the United States Military Academy at West

Point, New York, two years would pass before he saw his family again. There would be no vacation during that time.

The conductor opened the door. The June breeze carried smoke and cinders into the car. In 1911 there was no air conditioning.

It seemed strange that a great school like West Point would take in new cadets in June. Eisenhower knew that the time before studies began would be used to break in the newcomers.

"Tickets, please!" the conductor said.

Ike handed him his train ticket. It was almost two feet long.

The conductor looked over the tops of his glasses. "Going to West Point, eh?"

"Yes, sir."

"I went up there once to see the cadets. The Hudson River valley is one of the prettiest spots in America."

Ike put his ticket away carefully next to his money. He had in his inside pocket $160. He felt good about earning the sum which new cadets had to pay for books and first uniforms. He had also earned money for the trip. It had been hard work.

There was no money to spare in the Eisenhower family. Before Ike was born his father had gone to college for a time, had tried farming, and then had run a general store. The store failed, and money was scarce. So Mr. Eisenhower moved his family to Denison, Texas. This was lonely country, north of Dallas.

Mr. Eisenhower found that his job of working for the railroad brought in only ten dollars a week, and his family was growing. There were two young sons, Arthur and Edgar. On October 14, 1890, a third boy was born. They named him David Dwight Eisenhower.

When Mr. Eisenhower received an offer to work in Abilene, they moved back to Kansas. But his new job as a mechanic in the Belle Springs Creamery brought in little more pay.

Ike loved his dad. When Ike grew bigger he noticed that people respected his father because Mr. Eisenhower meant what he said. "When I'm grown up," Ike told his mother, "I'm going to be like Dad. He keeps his word."

One day Mrs. Eisenhower said to her youngest son: "David, we're going to change your name around. When I say 'David' both you and your father answer. Besides, I dislike nicknames." She was dismayed later when boys began to call Dwight "Ike."

The Eisenhowers soon had six young sons, and money became even more scarce. Mother Eisenhower was the person who managed what money they had.

She thought up things for the boys to do, insisted that they study, and held the family together. Her influence on each of her sons lasted.

When Ike was seven, his family moved into a large white house on Southeast Fourth Street. This house in Abilene had three acres of ground. There was plenty of room for the boys to play "cowboys and Indians." Abilene had been a famous frontier town in the Old West. In those days, Abilene was the town where the ranchers of Texas drove their cattle so they could be shipped east by railroad. Every boy in town fancied he could play the part of an Abilene sheriff, gunman, or cowboy.

The Eisenhowers, with Dwight at the far left, posed for this family portrait when he was eight.

There was room, too, for a barn and a garden. Ike and his five brothers spent hours weeding and watering the vegetables. Then they earned money by selling the vegetables in the richer sections of Abilene. The Eisenhower boys took pride in their work, and it took them about the town.

"I can sell vegetables, Mother," Ike said, "but it tires me out to hear the rich women over on the North Side haggle over pennies."

"There's something about every job, Dwight," his mother said, "that the worker doesn't like. But you have to do your best and not fret. It's sink or swim, and I want all my boys to swim."

Even though the Eisenhowers did not have much money, they were well-fed. They had a nice home. On Thanksgiving and Christmas they gave baskets of food to those who were really poor.

Central Kansas is rolling prairie country. It is a land where temperatures zoom to over 100 degrees in the summer. There seemed to be no let-up from the heat. In the hot months the Eisenhower vegetable garden consumed huge quantities of water. When there was no wind to run the windmill, water had to be carried in watering pots. There were chickens, cows, and a horse to feed. The Eisenhower boys earned money by mowing lawns. But when work was done, the boys cooled off by swimming in the Smoky

On long summer days Dwight (center) and his friends went fishing and sometimes camped overnight.

Hill River or in Mud Creek. There was time, too, to dig for worms and to fish for catfish or perch.

In the winter when temperatures were often below zero, the boys took turns splitting wood for the fires, carrying coal for the kitchen range, and lugging out the ashes. There were walks to be shoveled when the snow covered them like a blanket. And they played hockey on the frozen river with crooked branches instead of hockey sticks.

Occasionally, Mother Eisenhower let her sons cook. Ike liked this. Once when their parents were out, he and Edgar were making a pie. They formed

13

the dough into the shape of a baseball and began to toss it back and forth. Some fell on the floor.

Edgar looked out of the window. "Quick!" he said to Ike. "Here come Mother and Dad." The boys leaped to clean the kitchen, to smooth the dough into the pie pan, and to pop it into the oven. For a long time, how that delicious apple pie had been made was a secret between the two brothers.

Ike went to school with his baseball glove tied to his belt. He enjoyed baseball. It was fun even to play catch. He found that he could run faster than the average boy.

"I like both baseball and football," he told his mother. "I am the fastest halfback in school."

Young Ike (second from right, top row) was a star center fielder on Abilene High's baseball team.

"That may be true, Dwight," his mother said, "but I want you to be modest. As you grow older, you may discover that you can do some things better than other folks can. People will find it out soon enough. You don't have to tell them. Can you run as fast as Edgar?"

Ike laughed. "No, Mother, he beats me every time."

Ike's schoolmates liked him. He was a good student. He liked history, especially. He also stood out on the athletic field. He played center field in baseball, and he was a good football halfback.

The Abilene High School students were proud of their athletic teams, but they felt bad about their shoddy uniforms. They disliked having their athletes hook rides on freight trains when they played in another town. The students decided to form an athletic association. In 1909 few high schools were well-organized for athletics.

The students elected Dwight Eisenhower president of their association. He was pleased because it gave him a chance to help the school. He worked out a plan, and at a meeting he told the students: "We are all going to have to pay dues. Also, we'll charge admission to games."

The students agreed with him. They knew that raising money was nothing new to Ike. He had worked in the Belle Springs Creamery since he was eleven. At first he had to wrestle the heavy milk cans to the platform where they could be loaded into milk wagons. Then, when he became older, he shoveled coal in the engine room or worked on the platform winding a windlass to raise 300-pound cakes of ice for the wagons. His labor in the creamery had toughened his muscles and had made his body strong. He had also found out that to succeed he had to work.

The students knew that he was a leader. "Ike can make the athletic association go if anyone can," they told one another.

Ike Eisenhower was very happy about the athletic association. His program was a success. Later, other schools in Kansas adopted similar plans.

The six Eisenhower brothers—Arthur, Edgar, Dwight, Roy, Earl, and Milton—were a close-knit group. Their life was Spartan, but the family was a happy one.

Boys from the richer side of town discovered that when they raided the poorer South Side where the Eisenhower boys lived, they ran the risk of having to fight more than just one Eisenhower. Once Ike caught a bully beating up his youngest brother, Milton. Ike sailed into the bully like a tornado. The bully fell back under the fierce attack. Ike's fists pummeled the bigger boy as if they were the business end of a trip hammer. The word soon spread, "Ike Eisenhower can fight like a wildcat."

In 1909 both Edgar and Ike graduated from high school. They both wanted to go to college. Edgar, two years older than Ike, was particularly anxious to go to the University of Michigan to study law. Both boys got summer jobs on a farm and saved their money. But they soon saw they were not making enough.

"At the rate we're going," Edgar said, "neither one of us will get there." He felt discouraged.

Ike thought of a plan. "You go to Michigan," he said. "I'll give you my money, and I'll keep on working. Next summer we can both work. By that time I might have enough saved up so we both can be college students."

Edgar was delighted. "That's wonderful of you, Ike," he said.

Mrs. Eisenhower was even happier, not only because she would have a son in college, but also because Ike had been so unselfish. Her eyes glistened. "Dwight," she said, "I am glad you work so well with your brother."

In 1910 a friend of the Eisenhowers from the north side of town, Everett "Swede" Hazlett, began to talk about the United States Naval Academy. "It's at Annapolis, Maryland," he said. "Ike, they give you a free education. Imagine!" The more Swede talked, the more Ike liked the idea.

Ike again began to study. This was not easy, for he had been out of high school for almost a year and had lost the habit of studying hard. He was also working in the creamery at night. Nevertheless, he decided to take the examinations for both the Military and the Naval Academies. Then he found, to his disappointment, that he was too old to enter the Naval Academy.

"I'll concentrate on West Point," he told his parents. "I'll study as I've never studied before."

Mrs. Eisenhower and her husband had been raised in the Mennonite faith. The Mennonites stressed peace. So she was not pleased with Ike's decision.

The Mennonites believed in simplicity, self-control, and duty. It seemed impossible that one of her sons would want to go into military service.

"Mother," Ike said, "the way to peace in our country hasn't always been peaceful. Our country is not looking for a fight, but in this world we have to defend ourselves."

"I would hate to think of you in a war," Mother Eisenhower said.

"I want peace as much as anyone," Ike said, "and I'll do my part to keep it."

Ike's hard study enabled him to pass the examinations for West Point and to win an appointment. When he received the letter telling him he had the opportunity to serve his country as a West Point cadet, he was almost sorry to tell his mother the news.

He hurried home. He found his mother seated at the piano. She had had that piano ever since he could remember. He loved to hear her play. She was warm and gay. And her spirit entered her music.

She had heard him enter the house and turned on the piano stool. "Hello, Dwight," she said. Then she saw the letter in his hand. "I can tell the news by

the look on your face," she said. "You've won the appointment to West Point."

Ike beamed. "Yes, Mother," he said.

Mr. Eisenhower was happier. "I congratulate you, Dwight," he said. "I'm so glad you won the appointment."

Ike's years of hard work, his success on the athletic fields, especially as a football player, and his leadership as president of the athletic association, had given him self-confidence. "I'm sure I can make good," he said. "This is my opportunity."

He half closed his eyes as the train carrying him east rumbled on. He had read everything he could about West Point. Still, he did not know exactly what he would face.

2. In Cadet Uniform

Ike Eisenhower changed trains in Chicago. After leaving Albany, New York, he found himself in a coach filled with boys heading for West Point. There was little conversation. Each boy seemed alone, as if he were worried over the days just ahead.

The train clicked through country that interested Ike. Every once in a while he got a peek at the broad Hudson River. The blue water and green hills fascinated him. They were very different from the plains of Kansas.

Finally the conductor opened the door and shouted, "West Point!" Eisenhower grabbed his suitcase.

21

The boys started to climb the steep road cut into the face of the cliff. The granite cliff stretched upward for almost 200 feet. It was awesome.

One boy put his suitcase down. He gazed at the road leading to the academy. "My!" he said, "I'd like to hire a horse and buggy to take me up there."

Ike laughed. "It'll do us all good to stretch our legs," he said.

Ike, dressed in a neat gray suit and gray cap, looked at ease. But his heart pounded, and not just from the uphill walk. Starting a career gave you an odd feeling.

The next hour was one of the busiest of his life. He registered—signed his name in the register: "Dwight David Eisenhower." The date was June 14, 1911.

Barbers gave him the shortest haircut he had ever received. At the cadet store, tailors handed him a gray uniform. He made three trips from that store, at a run, to his room in the stone barracks. Heaped on his bed were the things he had carried. He had a rifle, a bayonet, a black cartridge box, a mattress, two gray blankets, a red comforter, a pillow, pillowcases, sheets, and a second cadet uniform. There was a full dress hat with a seven-inch fuzzy pompon on its crown and a brass coat-of-arms on its front that bore the motto of the Academy: DUTY, HONOR, COUNTRY.

He also had white belts, a brass breastplate, a brass

belt buckle, a can of brass polish, a pair of shoes, overshoes, rubbers, arctics, underwear, socks, handkerchiefs, and two laundry bags.

A voice from the bottom of the iron stairs howled: "Attention, all new cadets! All new cadets who have uniforms will put them on at once. Report in three minutes in front of barracks for close-order drill. New cadets who have no uniforms will double-time to the cadet store and draw them. On the move!"

Dwight Eisenhower felt proud as he pulled on his gray flannel trousers with a black stripe down each leg. The soft gray flannel shirt fitted him perfectly. He tied a flowing black tie around his neck and ran down the stairs.

At the end of an hour's instruction in marching under a hot sun, the new cadets were back in their rooms. Ike's roommate was John Dykes.

Because Eisenhower was in fine physical condition, the long hours at drill on the West Point Plain in front of barracks did not bother him. The new cadets were taught how to march and how to parade. They learned how to handle a rifle and how to execute the manual of arms. There was even a short course in table manners. On the target range down near the Hudson River the cadets learned how to aim and fire their rifles.

During off hours Ike enjoyed walking to Battle Monument at Trophy Point. The huge shaft of

Cadet Eisenhower wears his new "A" sweater at West Point.

Vermont granite carried in bronze letters the names of Regular Army soldiers killed in the Civil War.

The blue Hudson flowed far below, guarded by steep hills. "I've never seen hills like these," Ike said to himself.

In the distance Breakneck Ridge jutted down to the river like a tremendous saw. The river flowed around rocky Constitution Island. There was a dock on the West Point side. At this landing U. S. Grant and Robert E. Lee had come ashore to start their cadet training. Cadet Eisenhower was on historic ground.

A hundred yards away from the monument stood rows of cannons. These had been captured by Americans in the Revolution, in the War of 1812, in the Mexican War, in Cuba, and in the Philippines. The inscription on each gun told part of its story. "The part the inscriptions don't tell," Dwight said to himself, "is that Americans died capturing them."

The American flag floated from a white flagpole, far above the cannons and the elms sheltering them.

When the sunset gun roared, enlisted men who were members of the guard pulled the flag down gently. Dwight saluted. The bugles sounded retreat and sent their notes echoing through the hills. He felt a surge of patriotism. This was the flag he had sworn to defend.

After the middle of the summer, Ike's new roommate was Paul Hodgson. They became great friends.
Paul Hodgson had a slight impediment in his speech.

One evening after a September parade, the door
swung open and an upperclassman walked in. Both
plebes stood at attention. The upperclassman wore a
tight-fitting gray dress coat and white gloves. His
starched white trousers were creased to a knife-like
edge. A gray dress cap with a black, shiny visor
perched on his head.

"What's your name?" he asked Ike.

"Mr. Eisenhower."

"When you're spoken to, say 'sir.'"

"Yes, sir, sir."

"Where are you from, Mr. Eisenhower?"

"Abilene, sir."

"Where's Abilene? In India?"

"No, sir. Kansas."

"Well, say so. I never heard of the place."

Ike grinned. The upperclassman's peppery air
amused him.

"Wipe that grin off your face, Mr. Eisenhower," the
upperclassman said sharply. Secretly he was pleased
that Dwight had a sense of humor.

The upperclassman turned to Paul Hodgson.
"What's your name, Mister?"

"Mr. Hodgesson, sir," he stammered.

"Hodgesson? I thought you were Mr. Hodgson!"

"Yes, sir. I am."

"Well, which is it? 'Hodgson' or 'Hodgesson?'"

"The first, sir." Paul Hodgson chuckled. He knew the upperclassman was teasing him.

"Both of you plebes raise your chests up!" the upperclassman snapped. "This is no laughing matter!" Then the upperclassman took a shot in the dark. "Do you plebes play football?"

"Yes, sir," Ike and Paul said.

"I'm an end," Ike added. He thought he had a better chance at end than at halfback.

"I'm a back," Paul said.

The upperclassman scowled. "I didn't ask for your

history," he barked. He looked around the room. "This place looks like a pig's sty. Put it in shape. There's a room arrangement card on the back of the door. I want you to study that." Then the upper-classman walked out and banged the door.

Ike laughed. "My!" he said. "Speaking of pigs, he's as independent as a hog on ice."

"What do you mean?" Paul asked.

"He has a self-important manner," Ike said.

At the end of "plebe summer," school work began. The cadets marched to class in ranks. The plebes had a heavy study load: math, English, political science — beginning with the Middle Ages — surveying, and drill regulations. Both Dwight and Paul found the studies easy. They were well-prepared.

Eisenhower enjoyed being part of "F" Company in the Corps of Cadets. The company had unusual spirit. Its cadets were like a band of brothers with the plebes as the youngest members of the family.

The best part of the day for Ike came at four o'clock. Then, as he trotted out on the football field, he felt truly happy. With him were his friends: Omar Bradley, a tall, soft-spoken boy from Missouri; "Babe" Weyand, a husky youth from New Jersey; and Paul Hodgson.

After one hard practice, they were in the dressing room in the cadet gymnasium pulling off their football uniforms. Ike said, "Babe, do you think we can make this team?"

"I think so, Ike," Weyand said, "but first we have to overcome our social status of being just plebes."

The plebes thought this a great joke. None of them really minded serving an apprenticeship as underclassmen.

When football practice moved at a faster pace, Weyand carved a place for himself on the varsity. "The coaches tell me," Omar Bradley said, "that I'm too light. I only weigh 148 pounds. Maybe I'll grow." Dwight was disappointed because he soon found himself on the scrubs.

"Don't feel bad, Ike," a coach said. "We're well-fixed for ends. Let's see what you can do."

The scrub team reflected the spirit of the Corps. It battled the stronger varsity squad without letup.

Being on the football squad carries no privileges at West Point. The players live in barracks with the other cadets. They form in ranks at 5:50 A.M. with the rest of the Corps when the "Hell Cats"—buglers, drummers, and fifers from the band—sound reveille. Each player must make passing marks in his studies if he is to keep his football uniform.

Football was fun, but Ike also enjoyed life in the barracks. Once he and another plebe, Cadet "Tommy" Atkins were late at a formation. Cadet

"Tommy" Atkins and Ike were still plebes when this photograph was taken by Cadet A. M. Weyand in 1910.

Corporal Adler snapped, "You two cadets report to me in my room after tattoo in full dress coats."

"He'll punish us," Tommy said to Ike.

"He'll make us stand up straight against the wall," Ike said. "That's nothing!"

The bugler blew tattoo, a signal that in half an hour taps would sound. Then all lights would go out. The two friends started to put on their full dress uniforms—tight-fitting gray coats brightened by brass buttons and gray trousers.

"Wait, Ike!" Tommy's eyes sparkled. "Adler said 'full dress coats!' Let's wear absolutely nothing but our full dress coats."

"I'm with you," Ike said.

At the last notes of tattoo, Ike and Tommy reported. Adler was astounded by the almost naked plebes. Cadet Byrnes fell against the wall laughing.

Adler turned red. Then he shouted, "You dumb plebes...."

"Wait!" Byrnes said to Adler. "They carried out your orders exactly."

The next day word spread that New Cadets Atkins and Eisenhower were far too cocky, but many upperclassmen admired their nerve.

Being a plebe did not bother Ike. His sense of humor and ability to get along with people helped. He enjoyed being a West Point cadet.

3. On the Army Team

Ike and his classmates moved to summer camp at the end of their plebe year. It felt wonderful to be an upperclassman. Every cadet liked summer camp.

The cadets lived in tents to accustom themselves to life in the open. There were four cadets in a tent. It was a pleasant change from studies to learn more about military subjects. On the target range Ike liked the challenge of hitting a bullseye 600 yards away. He enjoyed learning how infantrymen patrol in the woods. He was impressed by the Tactical officers who trained cadets. They said, "Infantry wins battles. Other parts of the army help the infantry."

The camp stood at the northeast corner of the parade ground. It was a small tent city. The camp was laid out in streets, one company to a street.

One evening after supper, one of Eisenhower's classmates ran into the "F" Company street. His uniform was soaking wet. He had red brass polish smeared on the legs of his trousers. He was angry.

"Look!" he said to the "F" Company cadets. "Over in "A" Company they jumped on me. They said I was their prisoner of war."

The "F" Company cadets, calling themselves the "Tigers," declared "war" on the cadets in "A" Company, who called themselves the "Bear Cats." If a couple of Tigers caught a Bear Cat in the "F" Company street, they grabbed his hands and feet and bumped him against a tree.

The Bear Cats of "A" Company tired of this. One evening, Leland Devore, powerful football tackle and head Bear Cat, led an invasion. The Cats swarmed into Tiger territory.

An "F" Company cadet saw them and shouted, "Turn out, everybody! Here come the Bear Cats!"

The Bear Cats came armed with water buckets. They poured water over every Tiger they could find. The Tigers fought back with their water buckets. Then a cadet threw an open bottle of black liquid shoe polish. Another tossed red liquid brass polish.

Then someone ran for a "cot stick"—a stout stick that stretched the canvas on a cot. More cot sticks appeared. Eisenhower stood in the middle of the fight, swinging his cot stick as hard as the rest.

Someone yelled, "Look out! The Tacs!"

The cadets ran to their tents to avoid being reported by the Tactical officers who were in charge of camp.

In the fall of 1912 the "war" on the football field was almost as rough as the summer camp battle. The football coaches looked more carefully at young Eisenhower. At 170 pounds, he was a fast starter on hand-offs from the quarterback. Surprisingly, in

34

spite of his light weight, he had the knack of backing up a line. He became one of the best tacklers on the squad. Muscles he had built in the creamery helped him.

"Pot" Graves was Army's head coach. Captain Graves wore a turtle neck sweater, football pants, and a cloth hat that rose to a peak. He believed in rugged play. Because Dwight was fast and because he could stand punishment, he made the team. Captain Graves said, "I like the way you get off the mark, Eisenhower. You'll do."

But when the season opened, Ike was badly disappointed. Graves had him sitting on the bench. Nevertheless, Ike's play continued to improve.

His chance came against Yale. In a drive from Army's 27-yard line to the Yale 2, Ike carried the ball on almost every play. Yale could not stop him. The cadets in the grandstand were on their feet. They yelled so loudly the players could barely hear the signals. Then a penalty set Army back, and Yale won, 6–0.

At this time football players did not wear numbers. The next day when Eisenhower read the Sunday papers, he was annoyed. The reporters had confused him with another Army player, Cadet Leland Hobbs. They had given Hobbs credit for the 71-yard drive.

In the Colgate game, Ike starred as Army won. The

New York *Tribune* said, "The work of Eisenhower brought joy to the Army rooters."

A big game lay ahead. The Carlisle Indians from Pennsylvania were kings of the gridiron. Every fan knew of the powerful Indian athlete, Jim Thorpe. He was one of the best backs ever to don a football uniform.

Eisenhower hit Thorpe time and again with cracking tackles. The Kansas cadet shone also on offense. The New York *Sun* said, "Army has a rattling good back in Eisenhower...best man to carry the ball in the Indian game."

Then tragedy struck. In the next game, against Tufts College, Ike was carrying the ball. He had

Ike (fourth from left) and a few of his friends on the Army football team at West Point in 1912.

just dashed off a twenty-yard run when a tackler grabbed his foot and another tackled him head-on. A pain like an electric shock shot through Ike's knee.

He was placed in the hospital to rest his knee. When he got out he told the coaches he was ready to play.

Babe Weyand, at tackle, was the first to realize Ike was not all right. During a scrimmage Weyand heard Dwight groan. "What's the trouble, Ike?" Weyand asked.

Ike scowled and said nothing.

The next day, when the cadets went to horsemanship in the huge riding hall, the best riders practiced "monkey drill. " Ike was in this group.

The instructor blew his whistle. "Give me your attention, gentlemen!" he said. "Now the horses will be galloping. In this exercise, you throw yourself off your horse as you approach the low hurdle. Keep a good grip on his mane and on the reins. Then, as he jumps, you vault upward onto his back. These horses are trained. If you spring with the horse, he'll lever you upward. I'll show you what I'm talking about."

The wiry captain kicked his heels against the flanks of his horse and galloped in a wide circle. When the animal dashed toward the hurdle, the instructor slid from the horse's back. The officer's feet touched the

ground lightly, and in a twinkling he flew upward,
back onto the horse.

When the captain again faced the cadets, he said:
"Any questions? This isn't as difficult as it looks.
Is there anyone who does not want to try?"

No one moved. The cadet next to Ike whispered,
"I'd feel safer if the horse wore a saddle."

"All right!" the instructor shouted. "Lead out!"
Then he yelled, "Gallop, ho!"

The cadets tore around the ring. When Ike's turn
came, he slid from his horse at the right moment.
But the shock was too much for Ike's knee. He

let go of the reins and crumpled on the tanbark in severe pain.

The doctors in the Cadet Hospital spent four days working on the injured leg. The pain was far greater than it had been when the knee was injured in the Tufts game. "Tendons and cartilage are torn," the doctors said.

Colonel Frank Keefer, head of the Cadet Hospital, talked with Ike at the end of his first week in bed. "Mr. Eisenhower," he said, "I have bad news for you. You may never play football again."

Ike was terribly disappointed. But with the confidence and grit of the Eisenhower family, he said: "Sir, I'll be a cheerleader. I can also help coach the Cullum Hall squad—the scrubs."

"Right," said the colonel, "but your knee must get well. If it is still like this when you graduate, you may not be commissioned in the army."

Ike's world seemed to be breaking up. "If I can't be commissioned as a second lieutenant in the army, I'll seek adventure," he decided. "Perhaps I'll sail for South America—the Argentine," he told himself.

4. After Graduation

Two years later, with graduation from the Academy only a month away, Colonel Henry Shaw sent for Cadet Eisenhower. Colonel Shaw was now the chief medical officer. He realized that the first class cadet might go far in the army.

"Your knee..." the colonel said. "I'll pass you if you don't choose a branch of the army where you have to ride a horse. I suggest the Coast Artillery, Mr. Eisenhower. Here's a slip of paper to fill out. Put down your choices."

Ike knew the Coast Artillery had pleasant posts

40

along the sea coasts. But he felt it was not active enough. He took the paper and wrote:

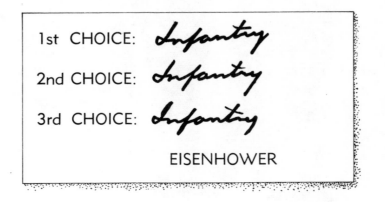

1st CHOICE: *Infantry*

2nd CHOICE: *Infantry*

3rd CHOICE: *Infantry*

EISENHOWER

Colonel Shaw grinned. "We'll see," he said.

As color sergeant, Ike thrilled when he carried the Stars and Stripes in the West Point parades. When June Week came and he carried the flag for the last time, he was both happy and sad. He was happy because he would be commissioned in the Infantry, and would have the opportunity to lead men under many conditions. But he was sad because he had to say good-bye to close friends.

On June 12, 1915, he received his diploma at Battle Monument. He ranked 61 in the graduating class of 164 cadets.

Back in their room, he and Paul Hodgson pulled on their olive drab uniforms. This was a great moment. They admired themselves in the mirror. Then a

plebe brought them a newspaper. Its headline read:

ANOTHER BRITISH BATTLESHIP SUNK

THE SHIP WAS TORPEDOED

"Do you think we'll get into this?" Ike asked.

"These German submarines are liable to drag us in," Paul said.

"War in Europe seems closer," Ike said. "You can almost hear the guns."

After three months vacation at home in Abilene, he took a train for Texas. At Fort Sam Houston, Ike went to school. The men at the fort worked long hours. Everyone was certain that the United States would be drawn into the war.

West Point had given Eisenhower a splendid education, but now he had to learn more about the Infantry. He said to himself, "If I'm to be a professional army officer, I will be as good as possible."

Off duty hours were frequently spent in nearby San Antonio. One evening he was introduced to a girl named Mamie Geneva Doud. The Doud family came from Denver, Colorado, but they spent the winters in Texas. Eighteen-year-old Mamie had soft brown hair, blue eyes, and a fetching smile. More important, Dwight found she was smart. He asked her for a date. They walked about the army post and enjoyed each other's company. Each delighted in the other's sense of humor.

The next day when Mamie came in, the maid said, "Miss Doud, the phone's been ringing its head off. A Lieutenant I . . . R . . . something keeps calling."

Every opportunity he had, Lieutenant Eisenhower came to San Antonio to see Mamie. If she had dates with others, he visited her family and waited for her to come home. Although he and Mamie were not engaged, at Christmastime he gave her a costly jewelry box. Finally, he persuaded her to marry him. She accepted a miniature of his West Point class ring.

One of the most important trips in his life came late

in June, when he traveled to Denver to marry Mamie. No other Eisenhowers were present. They were married on the first of July in a simple ceremony in the Doud home. Later, Ike and Mamie went to Abilene to meet his family.

The two were happy in their tiny apartment at Fort Sam. However, the war in Europe hung over them as if it were a dagger. They seldom talked about it, but both thought about it. The officers on the post studied the war news. It seemed to them as though the Allies—the British Empire, France, Russia, and Italy—might lose to their enemies—the Germans, Austrians, and Turks.

Dwight Eisenhower and Mamie Doud on their wedding day, July 1, 1916.

It was a dreadful war. Thousands of men lost their lives in the direct attacks in the mud of northern France and in Belgium. Untold numbers of men died in Russia, in Turkey, and in the countries of southeastern Europe.

On April 6, 1917, the inevitable happened. The United States, angry over the sinking of American ships by German subs, declared war on Germany.

When he came home that day, Mamie said: "Ike, what do you think will happen? Do you think you'll be sent to France?" She held her breath. She could picture him in the fighting.

"I don't know," he said. "I want to go. That's where I belong. I've been trained to fight for my country."

A few months later a great event happened in the Eisenhower family. Doud Dwight Eisenhower was born. But at the age of four, this baby died of scarlet fever. It was a terrible blow to Mamie and Dwight.

Suddenly orders came, but they were not to go to France. He was ordered to Chattanooga, Tennessee, and then to Leavenworth, Kansas, as an instructor for officer candidates. In March, 1918, new orders sent him to Gettysburg, Pennsylvania. "You will serve in a training camp for men in the Tank Corps," the message read.

Eisenhower was disappointed, but he consoled himself. "This is an important job," he told Mamie.

"I'm to teach soldiers about tanks, and I know precious little about them."

Tanks were a new idea in warfare. Leaders were using them to carry soldiers about the battlefield. Each large tank carried at least one heavy cannon; the small ones had machine guns or a small "one-pounder" cannon. The tanks were land battleships. Ike spent long hours at night studying everything about them he could find. He interested his men in the huge iron monsters by showing them how tanks were used in Europe. There was a problem — only three small tanks were in the Gettysburg camp!

On Sundays he and Mamie often explored the nearby Civil War battlefield. "I love this rolling Pennsylvania country, Ike," Mamie said.

"I do, too," he replied.

In November, 1918 the war in Europe ended. The Allies won, but every country that participated in the war suffered the loss of many thousands of men.

With the end of the war, the camp at Gettysburg was shut down. Eisenhower was sent to Camp Meade, Maryland to study more about tanks. Here he met Colonel George S. Patton, Jr., a brave leader who had been in the tank war in France.

One day after school, Eisenhower said: "I tell you what I think, George. I think speedy and powerful tanks can be used in large numbers. Tanks can punch holes in the enemy's line, so the infantrymen can rush through. This would save many lives."

"That's what I think, too!" Patton said. "The trouble is that the senior officers here don't agree."

When their new concept was heard in Washington, the older generals were angered.

One day Ike said to Mamie: "In Washington they call George Patton's and my idea 'treason.' General Pershing is sending Brigadier General Fox Conner here to check it out."

Fox Conner was a professional army officer and looked it. He was built like a fullback, yet he had the air of a kindly professor.

"What have you and Patton got here, Eisenhower?" he asked. "You have some of those infantry generals upset."

Eisenhower and Patton explained. Fox Conner said, "Tanks we have now can't move fast enough."

This was true, but it was the reason why the two younger men were so interested in improving the design of the tanks.

Eisenhower liked General Conner's relaxed manner and his quick answers.

When Conner told him good-bye, he smiled as he shook Dwight's hand. "Eisenhower," he said, "I admire your fresh approach to ideas and your common sense. We'll see each other again."

5. The Fox Who Could Teach

"Panama!" Mamie said. "When do we leave?"

"The orders say to leave as soon as we can get packed," Ike replied. "Now I know what Fox Conner meant when he said, 'We'll see each other again.' I'm to be on his staff in the Canal Zone as one of his assistants — his executive."

The Canal Zone is part of Panama. The great United States canal, cutting through the swamps and hills of the narrow isthmus, connects the Atlantic Ocean with the Pacific. The canal is important to ships of every nation, especially to those of the United States.

"The army's job down there," Ike explained to Mamie, "is to guard the Panama Canal."

When they arrived the Eisenhowers found their home on a lonely army post. The dingy house sat on stilts and it had not been occupied for years. Mamie disliked the heat of the tropics and their quarters. One evening, something from the nearby jungle flew into their home. It darted from room to room and swooped down, almost getting in Mamie's hair.

"Ike!" she shouted. "What is it?"

"It's a bat," he said. "I'll get my sword."

Mamie laughed as Ike chased the bat out of their home with flourishes of his saber.

The best part of Dwight Eisenhower's duty, by far, was his work with General Conner. Conner was not just interested in parade-ground drills. He also labored to improve plans for the Canal Zone in case of war.

Conner loaned him books from his splendid library. Often when Dwight went there, he found the general studying intently. He sat at his desk as if he were about to spring over it.

After the Eisenhowers had been in the Canal Zone six months, Mamie returned to her home in Denver to have a baby. While she was away the rickety old house was as pleasant as a tomb.

In July Ike took a short leave and traveled to

Denver to be there when their son was born. Dwight was very proud. He and Mamie agreed to name the baby for her father: John Sheldon Doud Eisenhower.

Ike had to return promptly to the Canal Zone. When Mamie brought the baby to Panama, Dwight never felt happier. "He looks like a football player," he told Mamie.

The Conners came to see John. "Do you think he'll go to West Point?" the general asked.

Ike laughed. "I hope so, General, but right now he's more worried about his milk bottle than higher education."

When he and the general were alone on the porch, the general said: "Eisenhower, in about twenty years

Young John Eisenhower, seen here with his mother, was a sturdy future candidate for West Point.

there is going to be a terrible war. I'm positive of it. It'll be the worst war the world has ever seen. Almost every nation will fight in it. It'll be far worse than the one that ended four years ago."

Eisenhower said nothing. A hot breeze from the jungle rustled the screens. He was not sure whether he believed the general or not.

"You'll be in the thick of it," Conner said. "The treaty that ended this last war won't hold the Germans. Japan is going to be powerful. She'll grab everything she can in the Pacific."

Eisenhower held his breath. When Conner spoke you had to listen.

"I'll be too old to help," the general said. He handed Eisenhower a book. "This is a book that tells how Napoleon and his armies overran Europe a hundred years ago. When you've read it, we'll discuss it."

As the days passed, Dwight continued to listen to the general. Soon Dwight Eisenhower believed what Conner had said: *There will be another world war.*

When Ike finished reading about Napoleon's strategy, Fox Conner said, "Now I want you to study the American Civil War."

After they had explored the problems of Grant and Lee and others, Conner handed Ike still another book. "This book," he said, "is by a Prussian general, Karl von Clausewitz. *On War* tells about total war.

It tells about strategy—how armies must be led if they are to win. It tells how plans must be made. Read the book. Then we'll talk it over."

In a few weeks Eisenhower said, "Sir, I've read the book."

"Read it again, Ike," the general said.

In another two weeks Ike returned and said, "Sir, I've read Clausewitz twice."

"Read it again."

Next, Fox Conner gave Eisenhower lectures on strategy. One day the general said: "Ike, I've a set of maps General Pershing used in France. Let's study them. You be General Pershing. Show me how you would avoid the trench warfare that bogged down the armies in the World War. Let's see how you would lead an army through France into Germany."

Finally, Fox Conner said: "Now every day I'm going to give you a problem about this army post. You write a field order—a detailed order—as if we were going to fight to defend the Canal. I'll give you a different place each day to defend or attack. You be the general!"

By the time Dwight Eisenhower's tour in Panama was over, he had learned a lot. He was grateful for Conner's interest.

Ike wanted to learn still more about the army. He hoped to attend the Command and General Staff

School at Fort Leavenworth. However, when he arrived in the United States, orders came for him to train men to fight in the Tank Corps.

Ike showed the orders to Mamie. "It's the same thing all over again with the same old machines," he said. "I'm disappointed. The infantry office in Washington says I can't go to Leavenworth, because I've not been to the Infantry School in Georgia. The usual custom is to go there first."

"What are you going to do, Ike?" Mamie asked. "I'll have to do as I'm told."

Suddenly a telegram came from General Conner, who was now Deputy Chief of Staff of the Army in Washington:

MAJOR DWIGHT D. EISENHOWER.
NO MATTER WHAT ORDERS YOU RECEIVE,
SAY NOTHING. DON'T EVEN BREATHE.
FOX CONNER

Quickly new orders came. Ike carried them to Mamie. "Hooray!" he said. "Please help me pack. I'm ordered to Leavenworth."

At the end of the year, Ike graduated first in a class of 275. "It was easy," Ike told a friend. "Conner educated me before I got there."

Now Dwight Eisenhower was sent to Europe with

the American Battle Monuments Commission. He took Mamie and little John along. They were in France for more than a year while Ike wrote a guidebook called *American Battlefields in Europe*.

During this time John was growing up. Ike and Mamie enjoyed picnics and sight-seeing tours with him. They visited the great battlefield at Verdun where almost one million men died. Eisenhower remembered Fox Conner's saying, "How could the generals in the World War have avoided having so many men killed?"

Dwight Eisenhower's next job was different from any he had had in his eighteen years of service. He

Ike, on new assignment in Washington, confers with General MacArthur, in 1931.

reported to General Douglas MacArthur, the senior general of the army, in Washington.

"Ike, I want you to be one of my staff officers — one of my assistants," the general said.

MacArthur, a most dramatic man and a brave battlefield leader, worked his assistants hard. It was Dwight's job to write the general's reports to Congress and his letters about important subjects.

But Dwight Eisenhower had time at home to relax. He enjoyed cooking.

"Daddy, what can I do?" John asked one day.

"You're on kitchen police," Dwight told his son. "You can peel the potatoes."

Dwight also took his son and Mamie about the city of Washington and to its museums and parks.

In 1935 the United States agreed to give the people of the Philippines their independence in ten years. Because of his vast experience, General MacArthur was selected as military adviser to the Filipinos.

It was a hard moment for Dwight when General MacArthur said, "Ike, I want to take you along as one of my planners." It was difficult because John, now thirteen, was in junior high. Dwight did not want to interrupt John's schooling.

Dwight Eisenhower kissed his family good-bye and sailed for the Philippine Islands with the general. He knew that adventures lay ahead.

6. The Hurricane Breaks

Not long after General MacArthur and his staff arrived in the Philippines, war broke out between Japan and China. The whole world was unsettled. The German dictator, Hitler, was preparing his armed forces for attacks. In Africa, Mussolini, ruler of the Italians, was slaughtering the Ethiopians. General MacArthur and his helpers worked hard to prepare defenses in the Islands.

"One of the first things we have to do," MacArthur told his staff, "is to find out everything we can about the Filipinos and their ability to create an army. What can we do to make it effective?"

Eisenhower met many Filipinos. Soon many of them became his friends. They warmed to his unusual grin and his kindhearted manner.

At the end of his first year in the Islands, Mamie and John joined Ike in Manila. It was splendid to have his family together, but Dwight worried, for the hot climate bothered Mamie.

Eisenhower read everything he could find about airplanes. He was interested in this rapidly developing military arm. He also took flying lessons.

"Your learning to fly worries me, Ike," Mamie said. "After all, you're a lieutenant colonel. Most officers learn to fly when they're lieutenants. You're forty-six. I think you may be too old to go up alone."

Ike grinned. "Don't you worry," he said. "Before I solo that two-seater, I'll know everything there is to know about it."

When he was sent up one day to loop the loop and do other stunts, his instructor said: "Ike, I've tied a sandbag to the rear seat. It'll balance the plane. I know you can do these acrobatics. When you have completed them in this test, you will get your license."

Eisenhower flew around the bay at 4,000 feet. The jungles of the Bataan peninsula looked like dense green thickets. Beyond them he could see Filipino farmers working in glistening rice paddy fields. It was a wonderful feeling being alone in the air.

Suddenly, after he started to do some simple acrobatics, the plane wobbled. It had never done that before. Ike worked at the controls. The plane did not respond. He looked back. The sandbag was loose. It was jammed against the control wires. The plane started to spin toward the water. He managed to reach back, and pulled the sandbag away from the wires. Then he headed for the landing field.

"I'm sorry about that," the instructor said. "But you kept your head. Do you want to go up again?"

"Yes, sir," Eisenhower said.

"I'll tie the bag more firmly," the instructor said.

Ike went up again at once. This time the sandbag behaved.

One of the things Dwight Eisenhower did in the Philippines was to select the site for the Philippine Military Academy. He said to President Quezon and to General MacArthur, "I recommend Baguio. The cool mountain climate will make it easier for the cadets to study." The founding of the military academy was another step in helping the Philippine people.

Living in the beautiful Philippines was like living in a tropical garden. But in early September 1939, Colonel Eisenhower came home early from work. He looked grim.

"You're home early, Ike," his wife said. "What's the matter?"

"Did you hear the news?" he asked.

She shook her head.

"Today Hitler's armies smashed into Poland. I think the world war Fox Conner predicted is starting."

A few weeks later Eisenhower said to General MacArthur: "Sir, I think it is time for me to go back to the United States. I can be of more help there."

"All right, Ike," the general said. "We'll give you the orders you want."

The Filipinos hated to see Dwight Eisenhower leave. President Quezon said, "Colonel Eisenhower, if you'll stay here and keep working to help our army prepare for the defense of the Philippines, we'll insure your life handsomely for your family."

"Thank you, Mr. President," Eisenhower said. "I appreciate the honor, but I think it is time for me to leave."

When the Eisenhowers sailed from Manila, General and Mrs. MacArthur came to the dock to say good-bye. The two officers had long been together and they respected each other.

"You've done superior work, Ike," Douglas MacArthur said. "The best of luck to you."

When the ship moved slowly from the pier, the band struck up "Auld Lang Syne." With more war news pouring in from Europe, it was almost as if the music were saying farewell to peace.

Colonel Eisenhower's new job was to train soldiers in California and in the state of Washington. "We are heading for a fight," he told the soldiers. "Our country is bound to be in it." But few believed him. Most of the soldiers thought that the United States would remain neutral. They laughed and, when they were by themselves, they called him "Alarmist Ike."

His son John was doing well in his studies. Both Colonel Eisenhower and Mamie were happy when one day John said, "I want to go to West Point and be a cadet."

"You must keep doing well in school," Dwight told his son. "That's the first step."

In the spring the war in Europe spread. Hitler's forces invaded Denmark and Norway. The British and French could not stop the Germans. By fall, Europe and North Africa were ablaze. Mussolini sent his armies crashing into Egypt and Greece. France was beaten into surrender by the Germans. Two thousand of Hitler's planes bombed Britain time and again. People in the United States read their newspapers carefully. They hoped the Allies would win the war.

Eisenhower, like other U.S. Army officers, worked feverishly to ready the army. Some members of the government were sure the United States would be brought into the war.

General McNair (center) and Ike plan strategy at the
Louisiana maneuvers on the eve of war.

In July 1941 Eisenhower, now a temporary colonel,
was sent to Louisiana to train large numbers of
soldiers who were soon engaged in mock battles. Ike
was chief of staff for General Krueger's 3rd Army.
There were some 240,000 men in Krueger's force.

General George Marshall, the Chief of Staff of the
Army, came from Washington. He was so pleased
with Eisenhower's work in Louisiana that he had
him promoted to brigadier general. Dwight and
Mamie were proud of the star he now wore on the
shoulder of his uniform. At the same time, both
realized his greater responsibility.

Tension in the world increased. Without warning,
Hitler's armies attacked the Russians.

Trade between the United States and Japan all but stopped. The Japanese thought they were treated unfairly. It was hard for Japan and the United States to understand each other. You could feel the hot breath of war.

General Eisenhower was stationed once again at Fort Sam Houston. John was now a cadet at West Point. He wrote his parents, "I look forward to your coming here to visit me at Christmastime."

On Sunday, December 7, 1941, Dwight came home at noon from his office. "Mamie," he said, "I'm dog-tired. I'm taking a nap."

At that very moment in far-off Hawaii, an event was happening that changed the life of every American. A fleet of Japanese warships was steaming toward the United States Naval Base at Pearl Harbor.

Without warning, Japanese planes took off from their carriers. They bombed the United States Pacific Fleet, as it lay at anchor in Pearl Harbor. Eighteen United States warships were badly damaged or sunk. Over 2,000 Americans died in this sneak attack.

In the Eisenhower home a phone rang. General Eisenhower answered it. When he hung up, he stared at Mamie. He hated to tell her the awful news. He knew that from now on their lives would be torn up.

"Mamie," he said, "it's come. We are at war. The Japanese have attacked Pearl Harbor."

Smoke billows from these American battleships bombed by the Japanese in the sneak attack on Pearl Harbor.

Mamie placed her hand on his shoulder. She felt as bad as he did. Later she said, "What about our trip to West Point?"

"You go without me, honey," he said.

General Marshall needed a man to head the army's War Plans Division. "What about that new general, Eisenhower?" a staff officer asked. Ike was selected.

In Washington Eisenhower worked a twelve-hour day and sometimes longer. The training he had received under Fox Conner and in the army was now invaluable. General Marshall consulted him almost every day. Marshall was pleased that Eisenhower always spoke his mind.

Not long after the Pearl Harbor disaster, Marshall sent for Eisenhower. On the walls of Marshall's big office hung maps of Europe and of the Philippines.

Marshall said, "Eisenhower, I want your thoughts regarding our best line of action. We have two main enemies. The Japanese are in control of most of the Pacific Ocean. Our friends, the Filipinos, and our soldiers fighting with them against the Japanese are in very desperate straits. Shall we send most of our army to rescue them, or shall we concentrate our forces against the Germans first?"

The office was as quiet as a tomb.

"Give me a few hours to think about this, sir," Eisenhower finally said to General Marshall.

Back at his desk, Eisenhower could "see" General MacArthur and his friends fighting in the Philippines. An officer placed a cablegram on Eisenhower's desk. It read:

TOP SECRET

Reinforcements needed in the Philippines if we are to withstand the Japanese. I urge the United States place first the war against Japan.

MACARTHUR

Once again in General Marshall's office, Eisenhower

explained his ideas. "We do not have the forces to defeat both the Japanese and the Germans at the same time. With our Navy badly crippled, we cannot reinforce the Philippines effectively. I think we must first defeat the Germans. If we don't keep them from becoming stronger, we will never win."

"I agree," Marshall said, "but we must help the men in the Philippines all we can."

Despite desperate measures taken by the American government, in four months the Japanese captured the Philippines. Americans felt as if they were in mourning. They could do nothing to assist the men who now became prisoners of war of the Japanese.

American soldiers begin the "death march" to Japanese prison camps. (Captured Japanese Photo)

The United States armed forces were still not ready.

Secretly, the navy began to transport hundreds of thousands of soldiers to Britain. Supplies of every kind were shipped and stored there. Britain was turning into an armed base for an attack against the Germans. But no one knew when the Allies would have enough trained men to cross the English Channel.

The fates of the two great English-speaking peoples were braided together. If one failed, so would the other. President Roosevelt sent a message of encouragement to Prime Minister Winston Churchill. Roosevelt used a verse of Longfellow's to show his thoughts.

> . . . Sail on, O Ship of State!
> Sail on, O Union, strong and great!
> Humanity with all its fears,
> With all the hopes of future years,
> Is hanging breathless on thy fate!

The hopes of the Allies were shrouded in fog. The path to victory did not stand out.

In late June 1942 General Marshall sent for Dwight Eisenhower. "Eisenhower," he said, "I want you to draw up an outline plan for defeating Germany."

About two months later Marshall said to Eisenhower: "I am convinced that the way to win is for an Allied army to cross the English Channel. The army must be strong enough to land on the French coast and fight into Germany. I wish you would go back to your office and draw up the orders for the top general we are going to send to England."

When Eisenhower had the orders ready, Marshall read them carefully. Then he said in his crisp way: "Eisenhower, get ready to fly to England. You are the general who will carry out these orders."

Dwight Eisenhower was rewarded for all the hard work he had done. At the same time, he felt the weight of his new assignment.

At home he packed as fast as he could. He told Mamie as much about his orders as their Top Secret label allowed.

"I hate to leave you," he said, "but I have to go. I face the greatest challenge of my life."

At the airport, with the propellers of the plane roaring up a storm, he kissed her good-bye. When the plane lifted itself for its long flight across the Atlantic, her love went with him. Also riding with General Dwight D. Eisenhower were the chances of the Allies for victory.

General Eisenhower and Prime Minister Churchill
were friends as well as allies.

7. Teamwork

The task Eisenhower faced was towering. How to defeat the immense armies and air forces of Germany and Italy was one of the greatest problems any general could have to solve. He was under great pressure. Friends warned him: "Allies have had trouble getting along since the time of the ancient Greeks, five hundred years before Christ. You'll need to see that everyone pulls together."

In London, Eisenhower found gloom. Radio news from North Africa said the Germans had captured a British stronghold.

Eisenhower talked to the great leader of the British government, Winston Churchill. He looked like a living cartoon of "John Bull," for he was short, fat, and had a jaw that jutted out when he struck a knotty problem. His people loved him. "Old Winnie," they said, "has more courage than an English bulldog."

"Sir," General Eisenhower said, "I'm sure we can win if we pull together."

"Teamwork, that's the answer," Churchill snapped. "If we don't have it, we will never defeat the monster Hitler or the jackal Mussolini."

Eisenhower asked that two young British officers be assigned to his staff.

"Check everything I do," he said to them. "Don't let me violate British customs or traditions. If I hurt the feelings of the British, we will never have team-work. When there is a job to be done, I want it done rapidly. But I do not want to disregard customs."

General Eisenhower called on the King and Queen. They had no idea of defeat. Then Eisenhower went to the areas that had been bombed by German planes. He was impressed by the damage, but he was more impressed by the spirit of the British people.

The thousands of American soldiers who were arriving from the United States needed more training.

Eisenhower told his staff: "See that our soldiers have areas where they can train, but more important, have them first meet the British people. Take our men on short tours of the bombed areas. The British have suffered, and I want everyone to know it."

Next, Eisenhower arranged to have British families invite Americans into their homes. "If we are on the same team," he said, "we must know each other."

Every kind of problem popped up. Once, when an American officer cursed a Britisher, Eisenhower sent for him. Ike said, "I don't mind your calling him a 'so-and-so.' But you called him a 'British so-and-so.' I don't want you on my staff."

General Eisenhower worked almost endlessly to solve problems about storing arms and ammunition; about finding food and housing for the newly arrived Americans; and about training men. In the training areas, he talked to sergeants and to young officers. He listened to their ideas.

He not only visited Americans who were in training, but he also visited British Commandos. These were special infantrymen who had raided German positions on the European continent. "I know of your bravery," Ike said. "Every American is proud of you."

Members of the two nations began to better understand each other.

General Eisenhower was sure that the fastest way to win was to send soldiers across the English Channel. But there were not enough American soldiers in Britain. The British army was too spread out—their soldiers were involved in India and in the Middle East. It would be over a year before the cross-Channel attack could be made.

In the meantime, the Russians were fighting tremendous battles with the attacking Germans. It was a desperate situation and important decisions had to be made.

Stalin, leader of the Russians, told the Americans and British: "You must land in Europe and fight! It will take pressure off us," he said. "The Germans will then have to fight you, too."

There were long but friendly discussions between the British and American generals. Roosevelt and Churchill entered the talks. Churchill thought that British and American soldiers should land in French

North Africa. He said that British soldiers in Egypt could fight their way to the west to join them. "If we do this," Churchill said, in his persuasive manner, "we will squeeze the Germans in Africa in a huge nutcracker."

Finally, President Roosevelt settled the matter. "Let's start some kind of ground action," he said.

This meant Africa!

One of the first problems that needed answering was, "Who will command the invasion of French North Africa?"

Military leaders on both sides of the Atlantic agreed on the answer to this important question. "Let's have General Eisenhower," they said. "He can lead Americans and British as a team."

Ike Eisenhower was now concerned about Africa. First he must select generals to head the invasion. He decided that these commanders would be the best leaders he could find, and he chose both British and Americans.

One of the generals was the dashing General George S. Patton Jr. This was the same man who had worked with him after the first World War when they learned about tanks. Eisenhower knew Patton, and said: "Patton is fearless. He can win battles."

The United States Navy played a big part in Eisenhower's plans. To have enough men for the invasion, soldiers would have to be brought from the United States to North Africa. German submarines in this 3,000-mile stretch of the Atlantic Ocean made this risky. To move the soldiers safely, the Navy assembled over 110 troop and cargo ships and 200 warships. The invasion was a gamble for high stakes.

Eisenhower ordered planes sent to airfields at the British-owned Rock of Gibraltar, at the western end of the Mediterranean Sea. He said, "The planes can then protect our ships as they near the African coast." He himself flew to the "Rock." He made his head-quarters in one of the numerous caves that riddle that amazing headland.

In French North Africa there was an unusual problem. No one could be sure exactly what the Frenchmen there would do. The Germans had captured most of France, and French soldiers in Africa were now thought to be friendly with the Germans. Some said that the French would lay down their arms as soon as the Allied ships appeared on the African coast. Others thought that the French would fight against any invader and might even fight for the Germans.

As the time for the landings in Africa approached, the pressure increased. Many radio men in the headquarters sat at their radios waiting to receive any messages for General Eisenhower. They could

receive but not send, for an increase in radio traffic might alert the Germans.

Eisenhower told a friend: "Drive me out to see the Barbary apes. You know the saying, 'As long as there are apes on the Rock, the British will control it.'"

"I know," his friend said. "Once Winston Churchill thought the apes were dwindling away, and he had some more brought in from Morocco."

General Eisenhower and his friend drove along a ledge-like road cut into the face of the Rock. When they found one of the tailless apes, they stopped the car. The wild animal hopped up in friendly fashion. Eisenhower patted the monkey on the head. "Wish me luck, old boy," he said. "I'll need it."

8. Fighting in Africa

The Top Secret code name for the invasion of Africa was "Torch." As the hour of the landings approached, it seemed to Eisenhower that "Torch" was a well-chosen word. A thousand things could go up in smoke. With almost a half-million soldiers, sailors, and airmen in combat, anything might happen. The biggest question mark was the French. On which side would they fight?

When "Torch" was being planned, General Eisenhower was advised by his helpers to contact General Henri Giraud of France. "If you can get him to go in with the expedition," they said, "he can tell the French in Africa we have come as friends. And

General Giraud can also lead the French in combat against the Germans."

General Giraud agreed to the plan, but it had been risky smuggling him out of France. The Allies sent a submarine to southern France to pick him up. Then an American flying boat flew him to Gibraltar.

Henri Giraud stood before General Eisenhower, tall and straight. "I am ready to command the invasion of Africa," he said.

Eisenhower stood speechless. Finally he said gently, "But, General, we look for you to go ashore and lead the *French* forces."

Giraud's gaunt face hardened. "I understood I

General Eisenhower and General Giraud salute during a joint ceremony in North Africa after the invasion.

would command everything!" he snapped. "I've taken great risks to join you. My whole family may be tortured by the Germans because I'm here to help the Allies. The honor of France demands that *I* lead the invasion."

General Eisenhower explained. "But I am the commander," he said firmly. Giraud refused to help if he could not command the invasion.

After the interview, General Eisenhower sent a cable to senior leaders in London and Washington about his conversation with Giraud. Back came the message, "We only regret you had to give so much of your time to this purpose...."

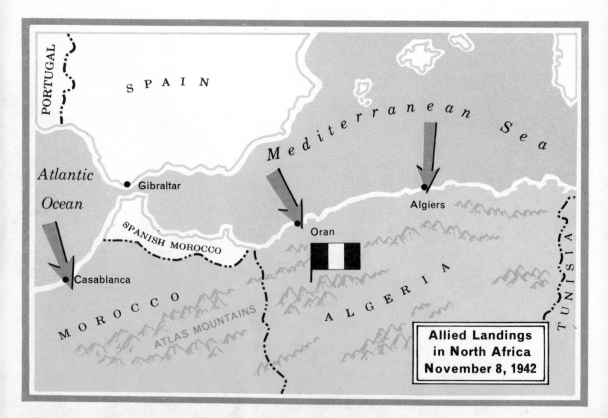

Allied Landings
in North Africa
November 8, 1942

Ike worried while he waited in the dank cave for news of the landings in Africa. The soldiers would soon storm ashore at Casablanca, Oran, and Algiers. Time dragged on. Waiting was a terrible trial.

Outside his office cave sat newspaper reporters. They were almost as hungry for the news as was General Eisenhower.

"I wonder if there is anything new?" one reporter asked another.

"Why don't we ask Ike?"

"That would only bother him," the first reporter said. "We all trust him. He'll give us news as soon as he can."

General Eisenhower walked about the cave. He smiled, trying to hide his tense feelings. He wondered how Mamie was. In order to mislead the Germans, United States and British newspapers had helped by carrying the headline: EISENHOWER ON TRIP TO WASHINGTON. So that his wife would not be fooled, Ike had cabled General Marshall: "Please explain the headlines to Mrs. Eisenhower. Tell her in strict confidence that I am at Gibraltar."

On November 8, 1942, Eisenhower woke early. It was impossible to sleep. This was the day the three vast Allied fleets would approach the African coast. Later in the day, the radios began to crackle. Reports of the landings at three widely separated places

American soldiers advance through the mountainous
country of North Africa.

trickled in. The French soldiers were fighting hard
against the Allies.

That day, Eisenhower sent for General Giraud
again. "General," Eisenhower said, "I wish you would
fly to Algiers. You can help both France and the
Allies if you can convince your countrymen we come
as friends."

Giraud had changed his mind and was now willing
to help the Allied forces in any way possible.

"I will go," Giraud said. "At once."

"Wait a minute, General," Ike said. Then he sent
for an American general, Mark Clark. Clark was a
capable and trusted officer who could speak French.

82

Eisenhower had known him since their cadet days at West Point.

Clark saluted General Eisenhower. "You sent for me, sir?"

"Indeed, I did," Ike said. "I wish you would fly with General Giraud to Algiers. Make every effort to get an agreement with the highest French authorities. Try to end the fighting! Also, we must get the French to help us against the Germans."

Mark Clark and Henri Giraud flew to Africa the following day, but they were not successful. The French there had no use for Giraud. They ignored him. Clark radioed this to Ike. It was a terrible blow.

Suddenly a radio operator handed General Eisenhower a message: ADMIRAL DARLAN IS IN ALGIERS.

This excited everyone in the cave. Darlan was the commander in chief of the French fighting forces. The French in Africa looked on him as their legal commander.

Ike gave instructions to General Clark at a conference in Algiers. Clark convinced Admiral Darlan to give the order for all French commanders to cease firing. Darlan followed General Clark's instructions. Then he tried to change his order, but Clark would not allow this.

After three days of fighting between the Allies and the French, the French ceased firing. THE FRENCH

ARE OUR FRIENDS AGAIN, a radio message said. General Eisenhower was pleased with Clark's work. Sending him to Darlan had saved many lives.

In four days the results were in. The Allies had seized 1,500 miles of the African coast. This cost the Allies some 860 dead and 1,050 wounded. Eisenhower had mixed feelings. The death of only one soldier would have been a dear price. Still, the landings could have cost far more.

The Germans were caught in a huge vise between the Allies in French North Africa and the British forces in Egypt. The trick for the Allies was to close the vise at Tunis where the Germans had their base.

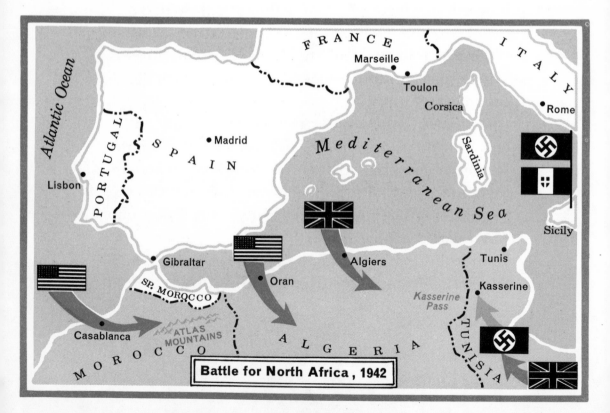

Battle for North Africa, 1942

Rolling westward across the sands of Egypt in their tanks came the "Desert Rats" of Australia. These famous fighters and the British soldiers marching with them were determined to squeeze the Germans out of Africa. "On to Tunis!" was their battle cry.

Eisenhower spent long hours in French North Africa visiting his generals. He told them: "We must hurry to close the trap on the Germans. We can't afford to let Hitler fly more men and supplies into Tunis."

But winter rains set in. The dirt roads became rivers of mud. The five hundred miles from Algiers to Tunis seemed like five thousand. It is a land of severe temperatures. When the sun shone later in the spring, the temperatures zoomed to 126 degrees. Then the African winds felt like air from a blast furnace. Soldiers living in tents suffered, and it was even hotter in the round-topped Quonset huts that looked like igloos.

Ike flew many times to see the front lines for himself. Once, when he wanted to fly to visit one of his leaders, bad weather set in. He was determined to go anyway. He sent for Sgt. Michael McKeogh, of Brooklyn, who helped him with personal work. He and General Eisenhower were friends.

"Just wanted to tell you, Mickey," Ike said, "the weather people say there are storms in the neighborhood. The air will be rough. I won't need you today."

Sgt. McKeogh turned pale. He said: "Sir, my mother wouldn't like this. She wrote me when she heard my job is to take care of you. She said, 'If General Eisenhower doesn't come back from this war, don't you come back!' I have to go with you on all trips, sir."

Eisenhower gave the sergeant his friendly grin. "All right, Mickey," he said. "Hop in the plane."

Friends told him: "Better give up these trips to the front. You just wear yourself out."

"But I get a first-hand look," Ike replied. "I enjoy talking to the men in platoons, and I get the feel of the situation from them. I always ask, 'Have you fellows figured out anything new — anything that will help the infantry?' "

In January 1943, the soldiers had more visitors. President Roosevelt, General Marshall, Prime Minister Churchill, and other British leaders flew to Casablanca, Africa.

It was part of Ike's job to take them around. They often traveled in jeeps. When Churchill raised his two fingers in a "V-for-victory salute," and when Roosevelt waved his felt hat, the soldiers cheered. No one was downhearted, even though at times the war seemed stuck in the mud.

General Eisenhower accompanied President Roosevelt
when he inspected the Army at Casablanca in 1943.

When President Roosevelt was alone with Ike, he said, "Now we *must* plan to cross the English Channel to beat the Germans."

"I agree, Mr. President," Ike said. He was glad that Roosevelt also thought this was the way to win.

At a January meeting in Casablanca, Mr. Churchill was in rare form. Mr. Roosevelt was not at this session of the conference. Churchill leaned back in his chair, puffed at a cigar, and blew smoke rings at the ceiling. "We ought to take Sicily," he said. "Then we can roll on up into Italy and knock her out of the war. What do you think, Brooke?"

British Field Marshal, Sir Alan Brooke, looked as rugged as his reputation. He was a brave fighter.

"If we are going to win this war," he said, "we have to make the Mediterranean Sea safe for our shipping. If we don't, we won't be able to attack anywhere." Brooke then blurted, "I do not want any important land attacks anywhere — at this time."

Churchill waved his cigar. He said excitedly: "I say, *take Sicily!* Then we can attack the soft underbelly of Europe! We can move up through Yugoslavia into eastern Europe!"

An officer standing at a large map swung his pointer beyond the Danube River to eastern Europe, then to the island of Sicily. Sicily sat at the "toe" of Italy like a badly fried egg. It is about the size of Vermont.

The Americans had been worried about Churchill's idea to move into eastern Europe. They thought fighting there would lengthen the war.

When it was General Marshall's turn to speak, he bit off his words. He spoke in a firm manner. "I think," he said, "the way to win the war is to cross the English Channel. Then we can fight through France into Germany."

"I'm for that, too," Churchill said rapidly. "But first let's knock Italy out of the war! We'd have one fewer enemy to fight. And, as Brooke said, we'll save shipping this way. What do you think, Ike?"

"Sir," Ike said, "if our purpose is to clear the Mediterranean for shipping, we ought to go after

Sicily. But to win the war as fast as possible, we must cross the English Channel."

Prime Minister Churchill blew a cloud of smoke at the map. The officer there stepped aside. "Sorry," Churchill said.

"Gentlemen," he continued, "things are going well here. The enemy could testify to that. I say we ought not to stop just because we have agreed on the strike across the Channel! Don't misunderstand us British," Mr. Churchill finished. He thrust his jaw forward. "We are *for* a cross-Channel attack! But we ought to take Rome, too! If we place pressure on Italy, she will collapse. Let's go in deep enough to make the Italians give up."

"I am sure the President will agree," General Marshall said.

Churchill stood up. The great leader of the British said: "Thank you. I am certain we are heading the right way."

When Mr. Churchill and the staff officers had gone, General Marshall said, "Eisenhower, I have news for you." He put his finger on the map at the place where the Desert Rats were battling the Germans.

"Here they are, " Marshall said, "south of Tunis. When the British forces and yours meet, someone will have to lead both forces. It is agreed that you will still be the overall commander."

Ike inspected the front lines. He worried. In some places the Americans were not ready.

Soon bad news poured in. Field Marshall Rommel, the "Desert Fox," sent his German Tiger tanks crashing toward the narrow Kasserine Pass. Fierce fighting took place in the rocky draws and gullies of the Pass and in cactus patches on nearby hills. For five days the Germans mauled the Americans.

A report from the battlefield read: "The U.S. Infantrymen have to be tougher. Our men were surprised. Many of the looks on the faces of our dead seemed to say, 'They couldn't do this to me.'"

This American crew trains its howitzer on the enemy at hotly-contested Kasserine Pass.

To overcome many of the difficulties, Eisenhower reorganized and strengthened the lines. The French were doing their part in the attacks against the Germans. The Allies were fighting as a team. Eisenhower especially emphasized unity. "We must be friends if we are to win!" he said tartly to his generals. "I insist on this. Pass the word to every man we have."

The Germans and Italians definitely lacked the teamwork and spirit of cooperation that General Eisenhower was striving to instill in the Allies in the fight toward Tunis.

Finally, after more bitter fighting, on May 13, 1943, the world was electrified. More than a quarter of a million Germans and Italians laid down their arms and surrendered. One of their best generals, Rommel, escaped by flying to Italy.

Eisenhower sent Mr. Churchill a message praising the part the British had played in the victory. Churchill read it in the English Parliament. The British leader held up two fingers over his head in his victory salute. He said, "This is not the end of the war, but is perhaps the end of the beginning."

General Eisenhower had shown, in gaining the victory, that he was a field commander and leader of the highest order. His superior ability and leadership served to weld the Allies into a winning team.

9. "You Won't Have a Friend Left"

Right after the conference at Casablanca, General Eisenhower began thinking about how to capture Sicily. He talked to one of his best soldiers, General Patton. "George, this operation 'Husky'—that's the Top Secret name for the invasion of Sicily. I want you to command the American army in the invasion."

"I'll be ready," Patton assured him.

First, Ike's staff planned the invasion. Ike approved the plans and gave them to his top leaders for study. Then, General Eisenhower called a meeting. It was held in Tunisia in a Quonset hut. The weather was hot, and there seemed to be no air in the little building.

"General," George Patton said to Eisenhower, "I've studied every airplane photo taken by our airmen. The enemy is depending too much on its trenches and forts. This will be ancient Troy all over again. You can't win a war by hiding behind walls. They'll find this out." Patton sat slumped in a chair near the huge map.

Ike grinned at him. "I hope you're right, George," he said.

Patton ran a hand over his almost bald head and smoothed his gray hair. "I'll bet I am," he said.

General Sir Harold Alexander picked up a pencil. This Englishman was known as a brave soldier who never became ruffled. He pointed to the place on the map where the British soldiers would land. Then he pointed to the narrow strait. "Sicily is the stepping stone to Italy," he said. "It's not too big a step across the water."

"Right!" General Eisenhower said. "Gentlemen, I want to impress on you one thing. As soon as possible after we land, I want the Americans and the British to connect forces and push forward rapidly. The more quickly we do this, the better for all of us."

"How about you, Matt?" Ike asked. "Are your paratroopers ready?"

Matthew Ridgway jumped to his feet. He was a leader with a tanned, hawk-like face and fine

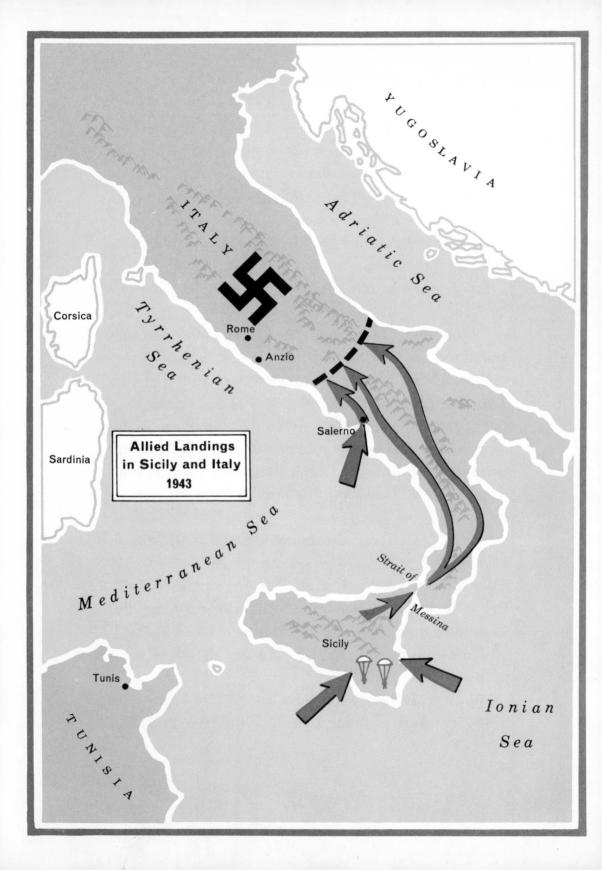

YUGOSLAVIA

ITALY

Adriatic Sea

Corsica

Tyrrhenian Sea

Rome

Anzio

Salerno

Allied Landings in Sicily and Italy 1943

Sardinia

Mediterranean Sea

Strait of

Messina

Sicily

Ionian Sea

Tunis

Sicily

TUNISIA

physique. Some soldiers called him "The Eagle."

"Yes, sir, General Eisenhower," he said quietly. "Our dedicated men can be counted on."

Sir Harold Alexander said: "The weather people promise us good weather. Let's pray they're right."

"How many enemy soldiers do you think are there?" Patton asked.

"Our people in intelligence," Eisenhower said, "estimate that there are between 300,000 and 365,000 German and Italian soldiers on the island. We'll come into Sicily with almost a half-million Allies."

Eisenhower turned to the experienced British admiral, Sir Andrew Cunningham. This pleasant-faced seadog had proven he was as great a navy leader as Britain's famous Admiral Nelson.

"Admiral," Ike said, "I would like the Allied navies to cruise close to the west side of the island. Pretend you are going to put soldiers ashore. Bombard the coast. A few hours later we'll surprise the enemy by storming ashore on the south side."

But the weather did not turn out well. Heavy seas pounded hundreds of ships carrying the soldiers from Africa to Sicily. Many of the soldiers became seasick.

To get ashore, Ike's soldiers used DUKWS ("Ducks") —truck-like vehicles that go through the water and roll over the land.

Ike's engineers surprised the enemy. The Germans and Italians had not guarded certain landing places, because they thought the water was too shallow. When the ships could get no closer, the engineers pushed "floating roads" overboard. These "roads" of steel looked like long narrow boxes, but they floated. Some of the soldiers marched ashore over them, landing at places where they were not expected.

The Allied airborne drop was not as successful as the ship-landings. High winds scattered the paratroopers all over the southeastern part of the island. However, this did confuse the Germans and Italians. They did not know exactly where the Allies would make their hardest fight.

But there was tragedy for the Allies. Anti-aircraft gunners on the ships, and some who were ashore, made a mistake. They fired at planes bearing the paratroopers. Twenty-three planes carrying U.S. paratroopers crashed, and almost one hundred soldiers died. British soldiers died, too, when they tried to seize a bridge. Allied artillery that was supposed to help them move forward became confused and smashed into their own team. There were not enough Allied planes on hand to protect the soldiers, so the German planes had a free hand. Bombs rained on the Allied infantrymen.

Ike watched the landings from His Majesty's Ship

Petard, a large destroyer. While the battle to get ashore was underway, some of the shells from the huge guns of the fleet smashed into Sicilian towns. Ike went ashore to see his soldiers and to inspect the damage. He was thankful that most of the towns and cities were unharmed.

It was obvious to front-line Allied soldiers that the Germans in Sicily were going to fight on. Thousands of Italian soldiers held up their hands. They were sick of the war and of their German allies. This news was rushed to General Eisenhower.

Allied soldiers, rifles ready, seek out snipers in the rubble-filled streets of Messina, Sicily.

"Fine!" Ike exclaimed. "Get this word to the Italians on every part of the island and in Italy. Tell them that their dictator, Mussolini, is bringing the war to Italy." He radioed the Italians: SURRENDER AND JOIN US. IF YOU DON'T YOU WON'T HAVE A FRIEND LEFT.

The Italians took Eisenhower's advice. Many more Italian soldiers gave up their arms. Italian citizens ousted Mussolini who fled from Rome.

It took thirty-nine grueling days for the Allies to capture the whole island of Sicily.

Eisenhower saw that the Allies must cross the strait into Italy and fight the German reinforcements sent by Hitler. The war in Italy became even more grim than it had been in Sicily. The battles in Italy were some of the hardest campaigns of the war.

In late November when Ike was in Italy, he received a radio message: PLEASE MEET ME IN TUNIS — ROOSEVELT. The President was flying back to the United States from a conference in Cairo, Egypt.

Ike flew back to Africa. He was worried and not sure of what the President wanted.

Eisenhower met the President at the Tunis airport. He was hardly seated in the President's auto when Roosevelt tapped him on the knee.

"Ike," Mr. Roosevelt said, with his wide grin, "I want you to command 'Overlord.' We'll keep fighting

General Eisenhower, at left, stops to talk to some British soldiers as he tours the Italian front.

in Italy, but 'Overlord' — the invasion across the Channel— will be our main attack now."

Ike said humbly, "Mr. President, I appreciate your confidence in me. I hope you will not be disappointed."

"I'm not worried," the President said.

"What about the Prime Minister?" Ike asked. "How does he feel about this?"

"He thinks you will win," the President said.

Eisenhower then wrote a farewell message to his soldiers. It was not easy to say good-bye to men who had fought so hard for him.

He flew to Washington for conferences. All the way across the Atlantic he studied plans for the invasion of Europe across the English Channel. He worked hard to improve the plans.

When the big plane circled the Washington airport, Ike felt happy, for he would see Mamie. His friend, General Marshall, helped with the family reunion. He gave them a private railroad car so they could travel to West Point, New York to see their son John.

At West Point the car was parked on a siding near the railroad station, close to the Hudson River. As Ike's visit was secret, only the Superintendent of the Military Academy, John, and three of his cadet friends saw Ike and Mamie. The Eisenhowers enjoyed a fine reunion.

On his flight back across the Atlantic to England, Ike again worked to better the invasion plans. The invasion across the Channel would be the biggest across-water attack ever staged in the history of man.

"It will be all or nothing," Ike told himself. "If we lose, the free world is doomed, and the Germans will win the war."

10. D-Day

In his plane winging over the Atlantic toward England, General Eisenhower studied his top secret orders. They read:

> "... You will enter the continent of Europe and, with the other united nations, undertake operations aimed at the heart of Germany and the destruction of her armed forces ..."

With Hitler in control, there was almost a "Dark Age" now in Europe. He had silenced criticism by everyone under his control. His weapons against the peoples of Europe were slavery, imprisonment in concentration camps and torture. The greatest across-water operation in history would challenge Hitler's stranglehold on Europe.

General Eisenhower faced his tremendous problem: How could he get an army — a large army — across the English Channel and lead it to victory?

Hitler had been unable to cross the Channel in 1941 and 1942. Now, in January, 1944, the task was even more formidable for the Allies.

For four long years Hitler's soldiers had labored to make the coast of Europe one long, huge fort. The obstacles along the beaches of the Continent were fearful. Airplane photos showed miles of barbed wire and thousands of German pillboxes containing machine guns sighted along the water's edge. Spies had reported underwater obstacles that could sink landing craft and, just inland from the beaches, deep tank traps and millions of mines. Powerful cannons also guarded the coast. And at places the Germans had flooded the lowlands. They had done everything possible to prevent the enemy from invading.

It was General Eisenhower's job to be sure the invasion would be successful. Fortunately, he had many dedicated assistants who had been working on the details of the invasion for many months.

102

The day of the landing of the Allied Army in Normandy, France, was named "D-Day." General Eisenhower tentatively selected June 5, 1944 for this vital day which meant so much to the free world.

It meant everything to most Frenchmen, too. They hated the German conquerors. The French "underground" — French men and women who were working secretly against the Germans — hoped D-Day would come soon.

On May 30 British Air Chief, Marshal Sir Leigh-Mallory, came to see Ike in his trailer headquarters near Portsmouth. Leigh-Mallory's face looked grave.

"General," the British air leader said, "I keep worrying about the paratroopers you ordered to

The leaders of the Supreme Command Allied Expeditionary Force meet with Ike to plan the invasion of Europe.

drop in Normandy. I feel it my duty to tell you I think they have little chance of survival. Therefore, I think it a bad mistake for you to send them. It will be a futile slaughter."

Ike drew a deep breath. He felt as if he were being torn apart. He knew the English air chief was brave, intelligent, and sincere.

"I think they will live—that is, the great majority will," Ike said. "Some will die. But those who live will be of immense help to our men landing on the beaches. The paratroopers can cut bridges leading into Normandy. This will hinder German reinforcements that Hitler will send. The paratroopers can cut German telephone and telegraph lines. We must stick with our plans."

After the air chief had gone, General Eisenhower went into his trailer to think. He prayed that he had made the right decision.

At four o'clock on the morning of June fourth, the news was bad. Headed by Captain Stagg, an able Scotsman, the weather specialists had a gloomy report. "Bad weather, General Eisenhower," Captain Stagg said. "We predict high winds and a very rough sea for the fifth of June. Landing in Normandy will be very, very dangerous."

Ike called a conference of his trusted advisers to decide what to do.

Captain Stagg reviewed his report and went on: "There will be low clouds. They will hinder naval gunfire. The observers won't be able to see."

A British admiral thought the seamen could handle the boats, but he was worried about the low clouds.

The British General Montgomery was greatly concerned over the confusion a postponement would cause. "I believe we should go," he said.

Others at the conference argued against such a stand. "The storm could wreck us," they said. "Some soldiers would be able to land. Others would drown with ships that are bound to sink. This would mean that those who do land would be cut off."

General Eisenhower went to his trailer to think the matter over. His army was on shipboard ready to sail. He could not keep 176,000 soldiers on board 4,000 ships without supplying more food. This meant using thousands of trucks. New plans would have to be made. He said to himself: "If I postpone the invasion a few days, the tides will change. That would mean that the sailors in charge of the small boats would not be able to see the underwater obstacles. Many boats would be smashed. If we delay, the secret of the landings will certainly reach the Germans."

Back with his staff, Eisenhower said: "We'll postpone the attack twenty-four hours. Rush word to leaders in the army, navy, and air forces."

At three-thirty the next morning, the storm was still whipping the English Channel. Rain beat a tattoo on the windows of the headquarters. It had almost the force of a hurricane. The conference was not a cheerful affair. Captain Stagg said: "Sir, tomorrow will be fair. We will have a period of good weather — for about thirty-six hours."

"And then what?" Ike asked.

"More high winds and rough seas, sir," the Scotsman replied.

No one said anything. Ike, sitting near a bookcase, stared into the fire. A few sparks crackled on the hearth. The wind moaned as if it were hurt. Sheets of rain slapped the windows. A few raindrops falling down the chimney caused the logs to steam and sputter.

General Eisenhower said: "If the invasion does not begin tomorrow, at least a half-month will be lost." He stood up. The tension was gone from his face. He said briskly to his leaders, "Well, we'll go! I rely on the courage of your men."

In the late afternoon of June 5, 1944, the greatest armada in the history of man started across the English Channel for the D-Day landings on June sixth. It was a gray day. Whitecaps crowned the waves. Out of every inlet, river, and bay in southern England steamed the invasion fleet.

American soldiers aboard an LCI headed for Normandy wait tensely for the invasion to begin.

Each ship took its place as in a well-rehearsed play. The ships formed three long lines. Because the Allied air forces and the Allied navies had played their parts well, no German planes or warships appeared. Late that night the soldiers on the ships heard the whir of planes overhead. They knew they contained the paratroopers, flying to their drop zones. The hopes of the Allies were sailing and flying to the Normandy coast.

"Full victory—nothing else!" was the order of the day as Ike visited his "sky soldiers" at Newbury.

11. Normandy

Before the paratroopers left, Ike had motored to the airfield at Newbury. At the airport he walked through the field where they were checking equipment. The faces of the "sky soldiers" were smeared with black paint, because they would fight part of the time in the dark. This and their tight-fitting uniforms made them look like ancient Mohawk Indians dressed in modern football suits.

They clustered about Ike. "We are counting on you!" General Eisenhower told them. "I want you to knock out bridges behind the German lines. This will prevent German reinforcements from attacking. I also want German telephone and telegraph lines cut. I have confidence in you. How do you fellows feel, anyhow?"

"I reckon we paratroopers will make out," a Texan drawled. "If we don't, I promise I'll have a job for you after the war. I'll let you help me rope cattle on my ranch. We won't get rich, but there's enough to eat in the work."

Ike and the paratroopers laughed. "I'll take you up on that," Ike said.

On the way back to his headquarters, Eisenhower thought of Leigh-Mallory's warning. "I'll be lucky to get a job on a ranch," he told himself, "if this thing doesn't work out."

A number of people had asked General Eisenhower if they could go ashore with the invading soldiers. They wanted to see the attack.

"Sir," one reporter had said, "when you go ashore later, may we go, too?"

"Yes," Eisenhower said, "but don't write about me. Write about the fellows who are doing the fighting."

"Sir," an aide had said, "I have to interrupt. Prime Minister Churchill wants to go on the invasion. He wants a fast answer. Admiral Ramsey's waiting for it on the scrambler."

Ike chuckled. The Prime Minister had insisted on this before. "The King has said that Mr. Churchill may not go, but he's still trying," Ike explained. "He has the instincts of a warrior. I want to go, too. But my place is here where I can direct the invasion."

Ike stepped to the secret telephone line and spoke to Admiral Sir Bertram H. Ramsey. "Bert, please head the old boy off! I know Mr. Churchill loves adventure, but tell him that if he became an accidental casualty our war effort would suffer. I have to refuse Mr. Churchill's request. I am sorry."

During the long wait for news of the landings, an aide handed Ike a newspaper. Its headlines read:

ROME FALLS!

Allies Winning in Italy

"Great news!" Ike said.

"Sir," another aide said, "here are the first

American troops move onto Omaha Beach to begin the invasion of "Fortress Europe."

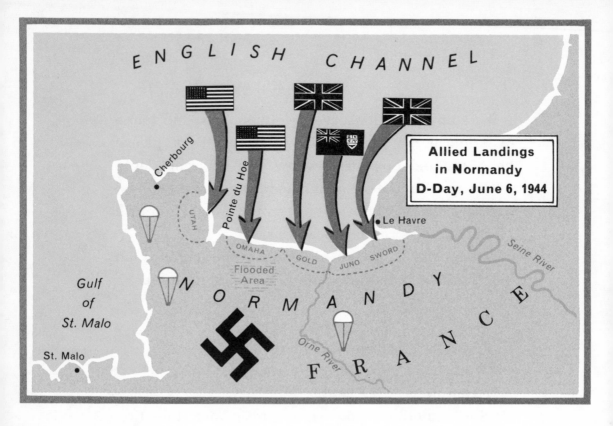

Allied Landings
in Normandy
D-Day, June 6, 1944

messages of the invasion." The room filled with staff officers. In the next room radio operators sat before their sets as if glued there. Ike turned anxiously to the relief map hanging on the wall.

"We are successful at Utah Beach and at the Canadian and British beaches," the aide said. "Our soldiers at Utah Beach are pressing inland and are fighting toward Cherbourg."

"Excellent!" Ike said.

The aide stopped. His pointer rested on the cliffs at Omaha Beach. "Trouble here," the aide went on. "The Germans have heavy weapons on the high ground. Our men are stopped. The naval bombardment of the shore before the landings helped, but we are being raked at the water's edge."

"Telephone call, sir," another aide said, "from Air Marshal Leigh-Mallory."

General Eisenhower took the call. Shortly he told his staff: "Leigh-Mallory says that the American and British airborne soldiers are successful. Only 20 planes out of 1,250 are not accounted for. The gliders carrying our soldiers met stiff fire. The number of casualties is unknown. Our paratroopers are scattered for miles, but they are attacking the Germans from behind." In a moment Ike added softly: "Leigh-Mallory says it isn't easy for him to admit he's wrong. But he says it gives him pleasure to do so. Any other news?"

"Yes, sir," the officer at the map said. He shuffled the messages. "The French 'underground' radioed saying that the Germans are definitely surprised by the landings. The German navy thought the water far too rough for a landing. In places, members of the underground are fighting the Germans."

"Here's a radio intercept, sir," a radio man said. "Hitler has ordered his men to die in place. 'There will be no retreat,' he says."

"I expected that," Eisenhower said.

The officer at the map said: "The second wave of

men is coming ashore at Omaha and is mixed with those that landed first. They are fighting to stay alive at Omaha Beach."

"Sir," another helper said, "here's a message from our Rangers at Pointe du Hoe." The officer swung his pointer to the hundred-foot cliff between Utah and Omaha Beaches. "Colonel Rudder reports a very difficult time. Heavy seas dashed some of the rowboats against the rocks. But the Rangers swam to the rocks. They managed to scale the cliffs, even though the Germans threw hand grenades down on them and cut many of the Rangers' rope ladders."

"Wonderful!" Ike exclaimed. "With bravery like this, we can't lose."

General Eisenhower was right. After fierce fighting at Omaha Beach, an infantry platoon finally wiggled its way into the German lines. Then a company followed, and soon a battalion. Finally, the Germans were defeated at Omaha Beach.

Long before dawn the next day, Ike left his headquarters on the English coast and boarded the *Apollo*. The destroyer sped for Normandy. When it arrived, his two principal generals came aboard for a visit.

The British general, Sir Bernard L. Montgomery, dressed in a gray sweater and his black tam o'shanter at a rakish angle, reported to Eisenhower. "Everything going fine, Ike," the little general said. His perky nose wrinkled. "I'm happy we are out of that jam at Omaha. The Americans are pressing on to Cherbourg. The Canadians and British are battling straight inland according to your plan. The air forces have licked the German planes, I am happy to say."

General Omar Bradley, steel helmet fastened tightly about his chin, peering kindly through his steel-rimmed spectacles, shook Ike's hand. Seeing this old friend was like having part of "F" Company of thirty years ago on hand.

"How are you, Brad?" Eisenhower asked.

"Fine," Omar Bradley said softly. "The worst is over. We still have to fight our way through the hedgerows."

Eisenhower worried about these rough fences. They were piles of rock and dirt dividing the fields. In the rows grew brambles, high hedges, and in some places, trees. The Germans who were fighting behind them had the benefit of natural fortifications.

"But," Bradley said as he smiled his wonderful smile, "I know we are on the way to victory!"

12. The German Salute

General Eisenhower cruised along the coast of Normandy aboard a destroyer. At every beach the commander came aboard to report to him. On the fifth day of the invasion, June 10, 1944, Ike went ashore to inspect. A staff officer gave him a brief report: "Sir, of the 152,000 men who landed on D-Day, about 11,000 were killed, wounded, or are missing. No one knows how many the Germans lost."

Ike walked with his staff along the beaches and through the huge tents serving as hospitals. Wounded men who were conscious were glad to see him. He saw the dead. Blankets covered them. He said to a friend: "Those feet sticking out! They emphasize the awfulness of war."

In the next three weeks American soldiers cut through the hedgerows and captured Cherbourg. Vicious fighting took place among the hedgerows.

General Elwood "Pete" Quesada came to see Eisenhower. This handsome young airman had a daring idea.

"General," Quesada said, "let's celebrate the Fourth of July. I have a fast P-51. I'll fly you over the German lines. This will give you a look at the situation."

"All right, Pete," Eisenhower said. "I'll go. I'm tired of looking at maps."

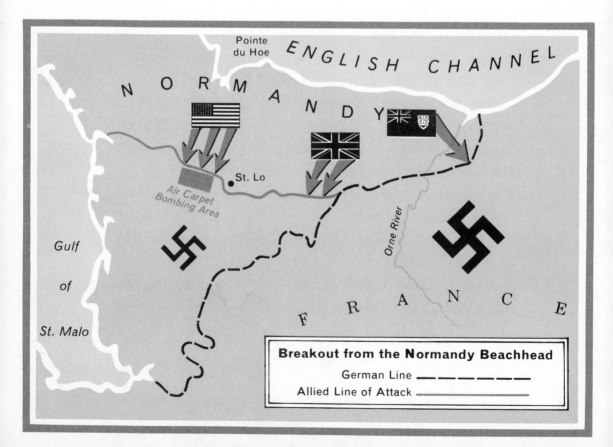

Breakout from the Normandy Beachhead
German Line _ _ _ _ _ _ _
Allied Line of Attack _____

Eisenhower saw the German defenses from the air. Obviously, the Germans were determined to keep the Allies penned up in Normandy. His mind flashed back to Fox Conner. In World War I, when the two long lines of Germans and Allies faced each other, neither could move. So Ike and General Bradley agreed on a new plan of action, and Omar Bradley sent a message to the airmen and artillerymen:

> "We must help the American infantrymen smash through the German lines. The best place to do this is near St. Lo. I want you to lay a 'carpet of bombs and shells.'"

The plan worked. However, some of the American infantrymen pressed so close to the "carpet" they were killed while the bombers were dropping their loads. As soon as possible, infantrymen opened a hole in the German lines, and American tanks roared through. "Now," Ike said to his staff, "we have elbow room."

Thousands of Germans were killed and captured. But many of Hitler's best soldiers escaped.

In England before the invasion had sailed, Eisenhower worked a trick on the Germans. He ordered Allied radio operators to send out fake messages. "Fool the Germans," he said. "Fill the air with make-believe messages. Make them think we have two armies ready to cross the Channel."

The Germans had swallowed the bait. So, when the new attack was ordered, the Germans did not rush reserves to St. Lo. Instead they kept many men back, waiting for the second army to storm ashore.

General Eisenhower knew that he could control the fighting better by being there, so he moved his headquarters to France. He repeated his previous orders to Generals Bradley and Montgomery: "Head toward the German 'coal bucket,' the Ruhr and the

British General Montgomery (rear) is shown here inspecting troops with Ike.

Saar in Germany. That's where the Germans make their weapons and ammunition. Capturing their factories is important if we are going to win this war."

He ordered his armies to move as fast as possible on a broad front across France. General Montgomery thought this a mistake. "I do not like your idea," Montgomery said sharply. "We can fight much better if our forces are concentrated."

General Eisenhower refused to become excited. He said gently to the testy British leader, "I am sure that if we spread out on all roads we can go faster."

Ike's plan succeeded. In two amazing weeks his armies swept through France.

The Allies now sent soldiers that could be spared from Italy. They landed in southern France. These were also placed under Eisenhower's generalship.

The hard-pressed Germans retreated behind the West Wall on Germany's western border. They had miles of barbed wire and countless high explosive mines guarding their big guns. They also had large concrete pillars, called "dragons' teeth" in the fields to block the tanks.

Eisenhower and Bradley knew the Allied line was stretched thin. They conferred, and Ike pointed out a spot on the map marked "The Ardennes."

"We are taking a risk here," Ike said to his friend.

"I agree," Omar Bradley said. "But we can't be

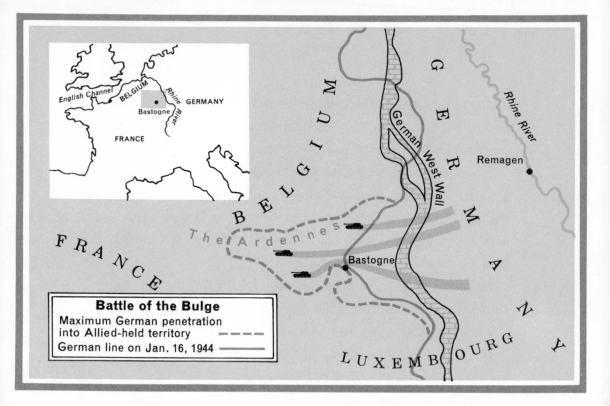

Battle of the Bulge

Maximum German penetration into Allied-held territory	– – – – –
German line on Jan. 16, 1944	—————

strong everywhere. We haven't enough men. Let's press on and crack their West Wall."

But behind the West Wall the Germans were planning a surprise. They brought three armies into the gloomy forest. Fog helped them keep this a secret. Allied planes could not fly because of the murky weather. Hitler had decided to make an all-out gamble. He might lose the war if his thrust through the forest failed.

On December 16, 1944 General Marshall sent Ike word that he had been promoted to the rare rank of "five star general."

Eisenhower had hardly pinned on his new insignia when bad news broke. Allied infantrymen on patrol in the forest spotted German tanks. They rushed the news to Eisenhower.

German infantry plunged through the forest. Behind them thundered thousands of tanks. Germans in American uniforms appeared at crossroads behind the United States lines. They gave misleading directions to American soldiers.

Americans fought for their lives. The Germans surrounded U.S. paratroopers at Bastogne. But the paratroopers did not stop. When the Germans demanded that they surrender, their leader, General Anthony McAuliffe, of West Virginia, replied "Nuts!" The answer delighted the Allied world. The Germans had no idea what "Nuts!" meant. But they learned, because the paratroopers fought all the harder.

While the battle was raging at Bastogne, Eisenhower assembled his generals.

"I can tell you what the Germans are after," Ike said. "They are trying to break through to the coast, to the Belgian city of Antwerp. They will go just as far as they possibly can."

Some of the generals showed their distress over the German advance. Ike said spiritedly: "I only want cheerful faces at this conference. Let's turn this attack into an opportunity."

General Eisenhower visits Generals Patton (right)
and Bradley (center) as he tours the Western front.

General Patton said, "Heck! Let's cut 'em off and
chew 'em up."

Eisenhower did something unexpected to stop the
Germans. He said: "General Montgomery, you take
the northern half of the battle line. General Bradley,
you take the southern half. Strike at the 'shoulders'
of the German attack."

This strategy worked. The German attack soon
halted. The stout-hearted paratroopers were rescued
at Bastogne.

The "Battle of the Bulge," as Hitler's desperate
gamble was called, cost Germany 120,000 casualties.
It hastened the end of the war. Soon Hitler received
even worse news. Huge Russian armies thundered
into Germany.

Bitter fighting raged through the winter. The Germans prevented Eisenhower's armies from crossing the Rhine.

Then, in March 1945 Bradley telephoned Ike. "I have wonderful news," Bradley said. "Our soldiers have seized a bridge over the Rhine at Remagen."

"Hold that bridge at all costs!" Ike shouted.

This was the beginning of the end for Hitler. Allied generals were happy that Eisenhower had not changed his ideas about advancing on a broad front. His armies surrounded the "coal bucket." German arms production stopped. Ike's men captured 300,000 Germans and freed thousands of Allied soldiers who had been penned in prisoner of war camps.

The Russians, fighting hard, pushed into Berlin.

American soldiers make a recording of action at the bridge at Remagen, now in Allied hands.

Their artillery shells bathed the city in a shower of iron. This was too much for Hitler. He shot himself.

The Americans met the Russian soldiers seventy-five miles south of Berlin. Eisenhower welcomed them. Then he traveled to the concentration camps where, with Hitler's approval, millions of civilians had been tortured to death. Many of them were Jews. Eisenhower made sure that all Germans learned of this unbelievable crime.

The Germans now sought out General Eisenhower and surrendered to him at Reims, France. The date was May 7, 1945. The cruel war had lasted almost six years. Now the United States faced the hard problem of defeating the Japanese armed forces.

After the senior German officer, Field Marshall Alfred Jodl, had signed the surrender papers, Eisenhower sent for him. It was two-thirty in the morning.

"Do you understand what you have signed?" Eisenhower asked sharply.

"*Ja, ja*—yes, yes," Jodl said. Then the German saluted.

Dwight Eisenhower, who had contributed more than any other man to the defeat of the Germans, felt weary. He told a friend: "I am so tired I could crawl into bed with a wildcat. But I feel as if a ton has been lifted from my shoulders."

13. "I Like Ike"

Before Ike crawled into bed, he faced a crowd of reporters. Members of his staff also pressed into the room. All wanted to hear from the general who had led the Allies to victory.

He posed with the two pens used to sign the surrender papers. He held them up so they made a "V-for-victory" sign. Photographers snapped pictures.

When the newsmen had asked all the questions they could think of, they hurried away to write their stories. Two remained to ask more questions.

"What single thing gave you the most pleasure during the last four years, General?" one asked.

"That's easy," Ike said. "It was rescuing Allied soldiers and airmen who had become prisoners of war. Fighting is hard, you know that, but being locked up and having no freedom and little food is harder."

"What did you like next?" the other reporter asked.

Ike smiled. "I guess it was the visit of my son John."

John had graduated from the U. S. Military Academy at West Point on D-Day. General Marshall, knowing of the bond between the Eisenhowers, arranged for John to sail to Europe on his graduation leave. General Eisenhower was proud of his new second lieutenant. They enjoyed a wonderful two and one-half week reunion.

A proud moment for Ike and Mamie was the graduation of their son John from West Point on D-Day, 1944.

When the time came for John to leave, he said: "Dad, I want to stay here and fight. This is where I belong."

"I wish you could," his father said. "West Point has given you a splendid education, but you need more training."

"I've had plenty of training," John said earnestly. "West Point prepared us. I've had most of the training I'd get at the Infantry School." John's face clouded.

Ike smoothed his thin blond hair. "It's not simple," he said. "If I let you stay here, others in your class would say, 'favoritism!'"

John did not reply.

"They'd call you the 'teacher's pet,'" Ike chuckled.

John's thundercloud broke. He laughed. "I guess I couldn't stand that," he said.

John went back to the United States for more training. But he did return to Europe before the end of the war and took his place in the front ranks.

When the word flashed that the war in Europe had ended, people wanted to see General Eisenhower. He rode at the head of parades in London and Paris. Millions cheered him. They were thankful for his courage and leadership. They remembered the teamwork he had instilled in the Allies.

President Truman, who had become President on the death of President Roosevelt, sent his private

New York welcomes Ike home with cheers and a ticker tape parade on June 19, 1945.

plane, the "Sacred Cow," so that Ike could fly to Washington.

"I never thought I would have this plane to myself," Ike said to his aide.

About 30,000 people crowded the Washington airport to greet him. In a few days he flew with Mamie to New York City. There, millions lined the streets to see Ike and to watch a parade in his honor.

It was wonderful to be home, and the very best part was being with Mamie again. But Ike did not forget old friends. He flew to West Point to talk to the officers and cadets. Then he and Mamie flew to Kansas City to see his mother. In her kind and modest manner,

130

she told her son of her happiness over his part in ending the war.

More Eisenhowers joined him in Abilene. There, boyhood friends stood with him and watched an unusual parade. Floats passed by showing Indians, cowboys, and frontier heroes of Abilene's early days.

Ike's friends began to talk to him about running for President of the United States. They knew that after a conference in Germany President Truman had said: "General, there is nothing you may want that I won't help you get. And that includes the Presidency."

Ike had laughed. He thought this a splendid joke. "I am a soldier," he said.

He flew to Europe to visit the Russians and to make friends with their top military man, Marshal Zhukov. But the Russian political leaders were not as friendly. It was hard for the Russians to understand American and British ideas, and vice versa.

War soon ended in the Far East, too. Now the Army's unusual and very capable war leader, General George C. Marshall, was retiring as Chief of Staff. People wondered who would replace him. Before Marshall left for his home in Virginia, he said to President Truman, "The very best man to head the United States Army is Dwight D. Eisenhower."

"I agree, General," Mr. Truman said.

When Ike was promoted to Chief of Staff, he and

Mamie moved to Fort Meyer, Virginia, not far from the Pentagon. His new responsibility as head of the Army meant long hours of hard work. Now that the war was over, the Army had to be made smaller to permit men to return to their homes.

Trips to foreign countries took him far from his Pentagon office. He flew to Mexico, Panama, Brazil, Canada, Europe, and to the Far East. People overseas responded to the warmth of his personality and his amazing friendliness.

Suddenly, Ike was offered the presidency of Columbia University in New York City. He took his time and thought it over for many months. Finally, he said, "I accept because I will have an opportunity to help young people."

He retired from the army and began his work as an educator. For this he accepted no pay. As president of Columbia, he started a study of wars and how they could be prevented. "Let's find out how war begins," Eisenhower said, "and let's study its terrible impact on people." He called this "The Institute of War and Peace Studies."

A few months later he started "The American Assembly." Reporters wrote about what General Eisenhower said: "This is the most important step I've taken as president of Columbia. This program will bring together businessmen, labor leaders, men who are prominent in politics, and leaders in the government. They will study methods for solving the problems that confront our nation."

He also started a major study of the use of manpower in the United States.

Despite all these projects, he was not too busy to see the young men and women who were Columbia students. He gave orders that his office door would be open to any boy or girl who wanted to see him.

He enjoyed watching the Columbia football team in action. When General Eisenhower stood on the sidelines at Baker Field with Lou Little, the Columbia coach, the players tried their best.

The Lions "roar" for Ike, new President of Columbia.

During this time Ike wrote *Crusade in Europe*. It is the story of his leadership in the Second World War. It soon became a best seller.

Two years after General Eisenhower went to Columbia University, President Truman sent for him.

"I must call you back into uniform," Mr. Truman said. "I have a hard job for you. I want you to fly to Paris and head NATO, the North Atlantic Treaty Organization. I need you as the commander of their troops. I know you can make the twelve countries of NATO pull together. I am absolutely sure that the peace of the world depends on the success of NATO."

"I accept, Mr. President," Eisenhower said. He liked the life at Columbia, but he felt he must obey the President's call. General Eisenhower knew that the twelve NATO countries had agreed on a common defense against any enemy. Communists in Italy, France, and Russia denounced NATO. "It is a pact aimed at Soviet Russia," they said. There were countless problems, Ike soon found, in making the United States, Canada, Great Britain, France, the Netherlands, Belgium, Luxembourg, Italy, Norway, Denmark, Iceland, and Portugal pull together.

The life was exciting for Ike and Mamie. There were quick trips to interesting places. But always in the front of Ike's mind was the necessity of making NATO as strong as possible.

134

It took him only fifteen months to join the many armies into one force. His thoughts for peace were evident. He said, "This is the first time a great allied army has been created to preserve the peace—not to wage war."

People in the United States began to talk of "Ike for President." Political leaders flew across the Atlantic to interview him. "We think you ought to run for President," they said.

"I'm not available," Ike answered.

But in 1952 friends entered his name in the Republican primary election. Thousands voted for Eisenhower. They trooped through rain and snow so they could mark their votes: EISENHOWER.

Ike told a friend, "I'm astonished people think I might become President!"

He flew to Abilene to talk to old friends. They urged him to run for the Presidency.

"Milton," Ike said to his youngest brother, "what do you think I should do?"

"I don't think you should run," Milton said. "You were trained at West Point to be a soldier. You are a wonderful soldier. I'm not sure you should be President." A few friends said the same thing.

But the movement to elect Ike kept rolling. Twenty-two newspapers, including *The New York Times* and the New York *Herald Tribune*, favored his election.

Publishers and editors believed in his ability to lead our country. They were sure he would be an honest, dedicated President.

Dwight Eisenhower gave long and serious thought to the matter. He asked Mamie for her thoughts.

"You must do what you think is best for the United States," she replied.

Finally, he decided it was his duty to obey the call.

A wave of excitement swept the country when people learned he would run for the Presidency. "I am a Republican," he announced.

The Republican National Convention was held in Chicago in July to choose a candidate for President. People from every part of the country gathered in Chicago to work in Ike's campaign headquarters. Many came at their own expense. The workers reflected Dwight Eisenhower's own enthusiasm.

On July 6 the Republican Party nominated Ike. In the huge convention hall, crowds went wild when General Eisenhower led his wife to the center of the stage and said, "Folks, here's my Mamie!"

"I like Ike!" buttons appeared. This became the campaign catchword. It was one of the most popular slogans in history. Everyone sang "In the Sunshine of Your Smile." It was Ike's campaign song.

He journeyed 51,000 miles by plane and train to talk to the voters. Newspaper reporters traveling with him

With Mamie at his side, Ike accepts the nomination
for President at the Republican Convention, 1952.

noted his earnestness and his honest speeches.
People rushed for the papers to read what Eisenhower
had said the previous day. They were especially
interested in what he had to say about Korea. There,
American soldiers were fighting the Communists.

In the early fall of 1952, Ike said, "If I am elected
President of the United States, I will go to Korea."
He explained he would fly there to see for himself
what was being done. "I have no magic," he said,
"but I want to end that war. Let us have peace."

Of the 61 million Americans who voted, 34 million
voted for Dwight Eisenhower. It was a landslide
victory. Thousands of messages of congratulations
arrived. Probably the one he liked the best came from
a captain in Korea. It was signed "John Eisenhower."

14. The President
Who Fought for Peace

"Fasten your seat belt, General Eisenhower," the crew chief said to the President-elect. "We are about to land in Korea."

The big plane banked. The flaps let down with a jerk. The speed of the plane slowed. Saw-tooth mountains, slopes dotted with snow, flashed by Ike's window.

General Mark Clark, who had fought so well in Africa and Italy, saluted him. General James A. Van Fleet also greeted him.

"Welcome to the Land of the Morning Calm!" Van Fleet boomed.

138

That is the Koreans' name for their country. But in 1952 it was far from calm. Korea had been divided into two parts after World War II. North Korea, backed by the Russians, was the Communist aggressor against South Korea. American and United Nations forces were supporting South Korea. People in the south, especially, had undergone much hardship.

Van Fleet gave Ike warm clothing for the trip to the front. Eisenhower, with his two old friends, toured the battle lines. The best part was when John Eisenhower appeared. He saluted. "Dad," he said, "I report as your temporary aide."

President-elect Eisenhower, flanked by his generals, Clark (left) and Van Fleet, tours Korea in 1952.

Men from the fifteen United Nations who were fighting the Communists greeted General Eisenhower. There was a happy outdoor luncheon, just back of the lines, with soldiers he had trained long ago. The temperature stood at below freezing, but the soldiers and Ike enjoyed each other and the food.

Eisenhower and Van Fleet climbed a steep hill after the meal. "Here's a pair of field glasses, Ike," Van Fleet said. "Look at those dark spots on that mountain across the valley."

"I see 'em," Eisenhower said. "What are they?"

"Caves. The North Koreans have cannons from Russia hidden in them."

Syngman Rhee, President of South Korea, welcomed General Eisenhower in Seoul, the capital. "It means much to my people to have you here," the old Korean said. "We are anxious for you to see what our people have gone through."

Rhee pointed to acres of flimsy shacks on the north side of the city. The Korean patriot said: "Almost a million of these people fled from the Communists. They would rather starve than be slaves. They have no other homes."

General Eisenhower was deeply moved by the plight of the refugees. He said, "I promise you that the United States will send you all the aid it can."

Before leaving for the United States, he enjoyed a

time when he and John were alone. It was hard for the father to tell his son good-bye. The general thought of the unusual danger John faced.

"If the Communists capture you," Ike warned his son, "they'll treat you unusually harshly. They'll think that by torturing you they can strike at me."

John answered in his quiet way. "Don't worry, Dad," he said. "They will *never* capture me."

Dwight D. Eisenhower became the thirty-fourth President of the United States in 1953. He started his inaugural speech with a humble prayer. Then he told the audience in Washington and the huge radio and TV audiences of his hatred of war. Every listener felt

Dwight David Eisenhower takes the oath of office to become the President of the United States.

Ike's sincerity. He reminded Americans of their heritage. Then he said, "Indeed, all free men must remember a soldier's pack is not as heavy as a prisoner's chains."

He had a feeling of awe when he walked into the White House for the first time. But his sense of humor bubbled through. He wrote later what he thought: "It is true. In the United States, any boy *can* grow up to be President."

Living in the beautiful mansion was something like living in a glass beehive. Newsmen wrote about President Eisenhower's every move. They even wanted to know what he ate. Mamie's days were almost as busy as her husband's. She had a house-keeping staff to help care for the 132-room White House.

President and Mrs. Eisenhower gave many dinners. Among the first guests were General and Mrs. MacArthur, former President Hoover, and Francis Cardinal Spellman.

Passers-by sometimes saw the President putting on a golf green built on the White House lawn by the United States Golf Association. He also liked fishing for trout on trips west. Reporters were surprised to discover that the President could cook. They smacked their lips over trout he caught and grilled over charcoal. They also liked Ike's "chili

Ike's young grandson David bows deeply as he shakes hands with the President before a golf game.

con carne," a spicy Mexican dish. He even baked a cake once in a while.

The President's work was far from relaxing. It has been said that the Presidency is the hardest job in the world. The toughest problem by far that President Eisenhower faced was how to deal with the Soviet Union, the leading Communist nation.

Resisting the spread of Communism without fighting is called "Cold War."

President Eisenhower and his advisors thought they saw a chance to break the Cold War in 1953. Stalin, the ruthless dictator of the Soviets, died. Now Ike hoped for peace. His hopes were dashed. Khrushchev, the man who emerged as dictator after

143

President Eisenhower, hard at work during his first term, signs a bill creating the Air Force Academy.

some months, was as difficult to deal with as Stalin.

The Korean War was uppermost in President Eisenhower's mind. He followed it closely. Thousands of Americans and their UN allies had been killed or wounded. Other thousands suffered in North Korean prison camps.

Suddenly, a new ray of hope flashed around the world. In July, 1953, after months of arguing, an armistice was signed. There was no victory, but the United States, along with its allies, had gone into the war only to defend South Korea. In this the United States was successful.

The President went on the radio. He said, "We have won an armistice on a single battleground—

not peace in the world." He told his fellow Americans, "The peace is not satisfactory, but it is far better than to continue the bloody, dreary sacrifice of lives with no possible military victory in sight."

There is no doubt that Dwight Eisenhower helped end the war. His visit to Korea made the Communists realize they could not gain a complete victory in that battle-ripped land. Eisenhower's vast military experience had also helped the United Nations forces.

The Korean War ended, but people knew that advances in science could bring total destruction to civilization. Hydrogen bombs—bombs a thousand times more powerful than atomic bombs—could now be delivered by jet planes or carried through space by rockets.

President Eisenhower worked hard to awaken the world to the perils of the atomic age. He was anxious that atomic energy be used for peace. He proposed that nations pool information on the atom for peace. The result was the creation of the International Atomic Agency. It was a giant step. The President said, "The atom, once man's slayer, will become his most productive servant."

In addition to the aggression in Korea, Communists were attempting to take over other Asian countries. Ike was more concerned than ever in his desire for world peace. He played a large part in the formation of "SEATO." This organization of eight nations was formed to combat Communism in Southeast Asia.

People all over the world listened to the President when he talked about peace at the Summit Conference in Geneva in 1955.

This meeting of the leaders of Great Britain, France, the Soviet Union, and the United States was held to discuss world problems. They hoped that they could, in this way, end the Cold War.

Ike captured the imagination of the whole world when he made his "open skies" proposal. He suggested that the two great powers—the United States and the Soviet Union—exchange military information and inspect each other's territory by air. It seemed fair enough.

Even though the Soviet Union would not accept this proposal, Ike had once again shown the world how much the United States wanted peace.

Business boomed in the United States under President Eisenhower. There was peace and prosperity.

But Americans received a shock in September, 1955. President Eisenhower was on vacation in Denver. At two o'clock one morning he said, "Mamie, I think I have indigestion." She telephoned for his doctor and close friend, General Howard Snyder.

The next day, headlines in every paper in America told of Eisenhower's illness. Big print in *The New York Times* read:

EISENHOWER IS IN HOSPITAL
WITH 'MILD' HEART ATTACK:
HIS CONDITION CALLED 'GOOD.'

Letters and telegrams by the thousands poured into the Denver hospital for Ike. Soon he was able to take up painting for relaxation. White House newsmen gave him a pair of red pajamas with five yellow stars embroidered on each collar tab. He

Painting at his easel was a pleasant way for Ike to relax from the cares of the Presidency.

laughed at the joke and good-naturedly put them on. He ran much government business from the hospital.

When his injured heart muscles had healed, he returned to Washington. Sometimes he and Mamie flew by helicopter to Gettysburg, Pennsylvania. There they had purchased a farmhouse. They both enjoyed the quiet Pennsylvania country. Ike had liked this country since 1918, when he instructed soldiers there in how to fight in tanks.

In early 1956 people everywhere wondered if Ike would run again for the Presidency. "His heart," they said, "will it stand another four years in the White House?"

He decided to campaign again, but two months before the Republican convention to nominate him, he had a painful illness resulting in an operation. "It was a real bellyache," Ike said. Fortunately, he recovered fast. Men and women close to him were astonished by his vigor.

During the political campaign, tension mounted in the Middle East. However, in the United States there was little friction. Signs pointed to another landslide election for Dwight Eisenhower. But he told friends, "If the people decide not to re-elect me, I surely couldn't feel unhappy about it."

15. Fifty Stars

He achieved the Presidency again — by the margin of 9,500,000 votes. This was 3,000,000 more than four years before. President Eisenhower was re-elected for a number of reasons: The incomes of Americans had reached a new high. People appreciated, too, the way he held down taxes. He was also highly respected.

Meanwhile, serious difficulties developed in the Middle East. In 1957 Ike gave Congress a grave message regarding Communism. At the same time he warned the Communist powers that the United States would not permit any further invasions in the Middle East. He asked for authority to send United

States soldiers to any country that asked for help against the aggressive acts of the Communists. This important program became known as the "Eisenhower Doctrine." Eisenhower sent a special ambassador to fifteen Middle Eastern countries to explain this doctrine.

Suddenly the Russians gripped the attention of the world. They scored a new kind of "win" in the Cold War. They fired the first satellite into outer space. "We call it 'Sputnik I,'" they said, "or 'fellow traveler.'"

Sputnik streaked through the skies, circling the world. It was about the size of a soccer ball and weighed 184.3 pounds. Its *beep-beep* sound seemed to warn of Communist ambitions. Then up went Sputnik II with a dog as a passenger.

President Eisenhower said, "This is not a race." Nevertheless, he ordered the space program to be speeded up. He organized an agency to insure that United States space efforts were coordinated.

Everywhere he went in the United States he was welcomed and applauded. However, he made one trip in the fall of 1957 where *he* did the applauding. That fall he arrived at West Point, New York, by helicopter, to dedicate a fountain in honor of his class, the Class of 1915. Afterward, he drove to Shea Stadium, near the Hudson River on the Academy's grounds.

He joined the crowd watching West Point play the University of Pennsylvania in "150 pound football." In this sport no player can weigh over 154 pounds.

He cheered both teams, but it was obvious his hopes were with the cadets, who wore gold-colored helmets and black jerseys.

He hurried to the Army sidelines at the end of the game. "Congratulations," he said to Coach Eric Tipton. "You have a fine team." He turned to the cadet players and shook their hands. "I got a thrill out of your victory," he said with a grin. "You know, I once wore this black jersey myself."

A football battle was a pleasant break for Ike, for in a few months he faced a grave decision. In July, 1958 trouble broke out in the Middle East. In Iraq, rebels killed the king and his son. In tiny Lebanon, mobs created turmoil. The disorders cheered Communists in Russia, and Nasser, dictator of Egypt. They hoped to control both Iraq and Lebanon. The President of Lebanon wired Ike an urgent plea for help.

Eisenhower asked his Secretary of State, "If we send soldiers to the Middle East, what will the Russians do?"

"I think," the Secretary said, "they will not go to war against us unless they believe it is to their advantage." But no one could be certain.

Great pressure was on President Eisenhower. The issues were not simple. Ike wanted peace with all his heart, but he believed that he must protect Americans in Lebanon and help its legal government —even at risk of war. "We have to do more than just want peace," he said. "We must do something."

Eisenhower moved fast. He ordered more than 9,000 soldiers and Marines, 70 warships, and many Navy and Air Force planes to Lebanon. His action prevented war. The situation in Iraq also improved. Small countries, worried about Communism, became heartened. The Communists were impressed. They realized Dwight Eisenhower was a man of peace, but that he had great courage. Soon, he was able to order the United States Armed Forces home.

The President decided to make a series of "peace" trips. He wanted to tell as many national leaders as possible about America's idea of "Peace and Friendship."

One of his tours opened with a visit to the Pope. Then he flew to Turkey, Pakistan, Afghanistan, and India. In each country throngs gathered to see "the man of peace."

In Afghanistan wild tribesmen almost mobbed him in their eagerness to reach his car. In New Delhi, capital of India, men, women, and children rode bikes, buses, cars, donkeys, and camel carts to the

Eisenhower receives a warm welcome in Afghanistan
as he tours in a horse-drawn carriage.

airport to greet him. Some also trekked along on foot.
When Ike's plane touched down in New Delhi at
sunset, he received one of the greatest welcomes
he had ever had. He rode in an open car through
crowded streets with Prime Minister Nehru. The roar
of the people sounded louder than the falls of Niagara.

His "peace trips" aided America but they were
not nearly as relaxing as were helicopter flights to
Gettysburg. Sometimes John and his wife Barbara
flew with him with their four children: David, Barbara
Anne, Susan Elaine, and Mary Jean. The Eisenhower
family enjoyed these delightful trips.

The President also visited the new Air Force Academy. The cadets in the Class of 1959 made him an honorary member of their class. He recalled he had helped decide that there should be an Air Force Academy. Then he gave the cadets some of his thoughts on living.

"You have the opportunity to create traditions here," he said. "True traditions give us some inspirations in our hearts. . . . Make sure you get enjoyment out of each day. Life should be things that you enjoy. Go to bed with a smile."

Back in the White House, Ike received reports telling of more trouble with the Communists.

In hope of easing tensions, President Eisenhower planned to visit the Soviet Union. Premier Nikita Khrushchev of Russia visited the United States. The President invited Mr. Khrushchev to Camp David, Maryland, where the atmosphere was relaxed, but few matters of importance were settled.

"I hope," President Eisenhower told friends, "that Mr. Khrushchev benefited when he traveled about the United States. He saw people living in complete freedom."

The President looked forward to his trip to Russia.

On May 1, 1960, the telephone on his desk jangled. A voice said: "Mr. President, this is General Goodpaster. We have a U-2 plane down in Russia."

The President said to the young general, "Give me the details, Andy."

"The pilot is Francis Gary Powers, sir. He radioed that his engine had flamed out. He was thirteen hundred miles inside Russia. That was yesterday. He hasn't been heard from since."

The U-2 flights had been going on for four years. They were the United States' method of guarding against surprise attacks such as the tragedy at Pearl Harbor. Powerful cameras aboard the U-2 planes could take photos fourteen miles above the earth. The U-2's kept an eye on Russian missile and rocket development.

President Eisenhower flew to a conference in Paris two weeks after Powers' plane went down. The heads of the United States, Soviet, British, and French governments attended.

Khrushchev hurled insults at the United States. He withdrew the invitation for President Eisenhower to visit Russia.

"I am responsible for what happened," President Eisenhower said. "I will take the blame." It was really not surprising when Dwight Eisenhower did this. He had been taught as a West Point cadet to accept responsibility.

Alaska had been admitted to the Union on January 3, 1959. Hawaii gained statehood on August 21 of

President Kennedy and President Eisenhower, deep
in thought, walk together at Camp David in 1961.

that year. Two new stars were to be added to the flag. The 49th and 50th stars did not represent these two states precisely. Congress had decided long ago that no star represented any particular state.

On the Fourth of July, 1960, the President issued an order that pleased him. The flag of the United States would now have "fifty stars"—one for Alaska and one for Hawaii, the newly admitted states.

When he put his pen down after signing the order, Ike thought back. Almost fifty years had passed since he left home in Abilene. He had served his country as a West Point cadet, as a soldier who became a five-star general, and as a President who fought for peace.

When Senator John F. Kennedy became President in 1961, Ike and Mamie left the White House for their farm in Gettysburg.

Gettysburg College gave him a splendid office on its campus. Visitors came from all over the world to see him. President Kennedy, and later President Lyndon B. Johnson, sought his advice.

Dwight Eisenhower had earned the respect of people everywhere. His amazing deeds, his search for peace, and his humbleness, have made him one of America's favorite heroes.

Index

A

Abilene, Kansas, 7, 8, 11, 12
Alaska, 155
Alexander, Harold, 93, 95
Atkins, "Tommy," 29, 30 (pic), 31

B

Battle of the Bulge, 122 (map), 122-124
Belle Springs Creamery, 10, 15, 16
Bradley, Omar, 28, 29, 103 (pic), 116, 119-121, 124 (pic)
Brooke, Alan, 87

C

Camp David, Maryland, 154
Casablanca Conference, 87-89
Churchill, Winston, 68, 70 (pic), 71-75, 86-89, 91, 110
Clark, Mark, 82, 83, 138, 139 (pic)
Cold War, 143, 146, 150
Conner, Fox, 47, 49, 51, 52, 54
Crusade in Europe, 134
Cunningham, Andrew, 95

D

Darlan, Jean, 83
D-Day landings, 103, 106-115, 107 (pic), 112 (map)
Doud, Mamie Geneva, 43, 44 (pic) *see also* Eisenhower, Mamie
DUKWs, 95, 111 (pic)

E

Egypt, 84, 85
Eisenhower, Arthur, 10
Eisenhower, David Jacob, 9, 10
Eisenhower, David, 143 (pic)
Eisenhower Doctrine, 150
Eisenhower, Doud Dwight, 45
Eisenhower, Dwight David birth of, 10
children of, 45, 50
in Korea, 138-141,

139 (pic)
marriage of, 44
name of, 10
in Panama Canal Zone, 48-52
in Philippines, 57-61
as President of Columbia University, 132-134, 133 (pic)
as President of the United States, 147-157
first term, 141-148
peace trips, 152, 153
second term, 149-157
space program, 150
presidential campaign of, 135-137 (pic)
promotions of, 63, 131, 133
as Tank Corps instructor, 45, 46
at West Point, 21-42
in World War II, 71-126
Eisenhower, Edgar, 10, 13, 14, 17
Eisenhower, Ida, 10-12, 15, 17-20
Eisenhower, John Sheldon Doud, 50 (pic), 56, 62, 100, 128 (pic), 129, 139, 141
Eisenhower, Mamie, 45, 46, 49, 50 (pic), 58, 128 (pic), 130, 137 (pic)
Eisenhower, Milton, 16, 135
English Channel, 68, 87-89, 99, 100, 102, 105 (pic), 106

F

Fort Sam Houston, 42
French, 76, 78, 82, 83

G

Geneva Summit Conference, 146
Germans, 62, 67, 71, 76, 84, 112-126
surrender at Reims, 126
Gettysburg, Pennsylvania, 45, 46, 148, 157
Gibraltar, 76, 77
Giraud, Henri, 78, 79

(pic), 80, 82, 83
Graves, "Pot," 35

H

Hazlett, Everett "Swede," 17
Hawaii, 155
Hitler, Adolf, 57, 60, 62, 63, 101, 102, 122, 124-126
Hodgson, Paul, 26-28, 41, 42
"Husky," *see* Sicily, landings in

I

International Atomic Agency, 145
Italy, 98, 99 (pic)
invasion of, 94 (map)

J

Japan, 51, 57, 64
Jodl, Alfred, 126

K

Kasserine Pass, 90 (pic)
Keefer, Frank, 39
Kennedy, John F., 156 (pic), 157
Khrushchev, Nikita, 143, 154
Korea, 137-141, 144, 145

L

Lebanon, 151, 152
Leigh-Mallory, Trafford, 103 (pic), 104, 113

M

MacArthur, Douglas, 55 (pic), 56, 57, 60, 61
Marshall, George, 63, 65-69, 88, 89, 131
McKeogh, Michael, 85, 86
Messina, Italy, 97 (pic)
Middle East, 148-152
Montgomery, Bernard L., 103 (pic), 105, 115, 120 (pic), 121
Mussolini, Benito, 57, 62, 98

N

NATO, 134
Normandy, France, 103, 104, 117
breakout from, 118 (map), 118-120

North Africa, 75, 76, 81, 82 (pic), 84 (map), 85
landings in, 78-82, 80 (map)

O

Omaha Beach, 111 (pic), 112, 115
"Overlord," see D-Day landings

P

Panama Canal Zone, 48, 50, 52
Paratroopers, 92 (pic), 96, 104, 107, 108 (pic), 109, 110
Patton, George S., 46, 47, 75, 92, 93, 124 (pic)
Pearl Harbor, 64, 65 (pic)
Philippine Islands, 56-60, 66, 67
Philippine Military Academy, 60
Powers, Francis Gary, 155

Q

Quesada, Elwood "Pete," 118

R

Ramsey, Bertram, 103 (pic), 110, 111
Reims, France, 126
Remagen Bridge, 125 (pic)
Rhee, Syngman, 140
Ridgway, Matthew, 93
Rommel, Erwin, 90, 91
Roosevelt, Franklin D., 68, 74, 75, 86, 87 (pic), 98, 99
Russia, see Soviet Union

S

SEATO, 146
Shaw, Henry, 40
Sicily, 88, 92, 93
landings in, 94 (map), 95-98
Soviet Union, 63, 74, 124-126, 143, 146, 150, 151, 154
Sputnik, 150
Summit Conference, 146
Supreme Command Allied Expeditionary Force, 103 (pic)
Surrender of Germans and Italians, 91

T

Tedder, Arthur, 103 (pic)
"Torch," see North Africa, landings in
Tunis, 84, 85, 89, 91
Truman, Harry S., 129, 131, 134

U

U-2 incident, 154, 155
United States Naval Academy, 17, 18
United States Military Academy, 8, 18, 21-37

V

Van Fleet, James, 138, 139 (pic), 140

W

Weyand, A. M. "Babe," 28, 29, 37
West Point, see United States Military Academy
World War I, 45, 46
World War II, Eisenhower in, 71-126

ABOUT THE AUTHOR

Col. "Red" Reeder has been associated with the Army all his life. He was an outstanding athlete at West Point, and directed athletics for the Army for two years in the Canal Zone. In 1942 he was sent by General Marshall to New Guinea and Guadalcanal. More than one million copies of his report of this trip were printed and used as training manuals by every division in the United States, by the British in Africa, and by West Point Cadets.

Col. Reeder's military service extended until his retirement in 1947. He led a regiment ashore in Normandy on D-Day and was seriously wounded on the sixth day of the invasion. For 20 years he was Special Assistant to the Director of Athletics at West Point. He is the author of more than 24 books.